# AN INTRODUCTION TO
# CORPORATE FINANCE

# The Securities & Investment Institute

Mission Statement:

> *To set standards of professional excellence and integrity for the investment and securities industry, providing qualifications and promoting the highest level of competence to our members, other individuals and firms.*

The Securities and Investment Institute is the UK's leading professional and membership body for practitioners in the securities and investment industry, with more than 16,000 members with an increasing number working outside the UK. It is also the major examining body for the industry, with a full range of qualifications aimed at people entering and working in it. More than 30,000 examinations are taken annually in more than 30 countries.

You can contact us through our website *www.sii.org.uk*

Our membership believes that keeping up to date is central to professional development. We are delighted to endorse the Wiley/SII publishing partnership and recommend this series of books to our members and all those who work in the industry.

**Ruth Martin**
Managing Director

# AN INTRODUCTION TO CORPORATE FINANCE

## TRANSACTIONS AND TECHNIQUES

### Second Edition

....................................

Ross Geddes

JOHN WILEY & SONS, LTD

*For*
*Alexander, Clare, Colin, Ellery and Gillian*

# CONTENTS

# ABOUT THE AUTHOR

. . . . . . . . . . . . . . . . . . . . . . . . . . . . . . . . . . . . . . .

Ross Geddes is a practitioner and educator in the corporate finance world. He has over 20 years of experience working on financings (both debt and equity) as well as M&A transactions. During his corporate finance career in Canada and the UK, he helped corporations and governments raise over $7 billion in equity in IPOs, secondary offerings and privatisations. Ross is the author of three other books on finance. He now resides in Canada.

# Chapter

# 1

. . . . . . . . . . . . . . . . . . . . . . . . . . . . . . . . .

# 'BEHIND THE CHINESE WALL'

**corporate** *adj.* 1. forming a corporation; 2. forming one body of many individuals; 3. of or belonging to a corporation or group.

**finance** *noun* 1. the management of (esp public) money; 2. monetary support for an enterprise; 3 (in pl) the money resources of a state, company, or person.

*The Oxford English Dictionary*, 2nd Edition, 1989
by permission of Oxford University Press

Thus, *corporate finance* – a phrase relating to how companies obtain and use finance to grow their business. In the City, on Wall Street and wherever banks and investment banks congregate, corporate finance takes on a specific meaning.

This book has three goals: to provide a description of some of the major corporate finance transactions; to describe the role of corporate financiers in such transactions; and to introduce the main valuation tools used in the transactions.

## CORPORATE FINANCE IN INVESTMENT BANKING

Corporate finance tends to become more narrowly focused when one talks to an investment banker or investment bank. Corporate finance departments advertise their abilities to provide advice and complete transactions in the following areas:

- Mergers, Acquisitions and Divestitures (*M&A*).
- Financial Advice (capital structure and fairness opinions).
- Flotations/Initial Public Offerings (*IPOs*).
- Further Equity Offerings.

Note that the last two in the list, relating to equity fundraising, are often placed in a separate department called Equity Capital Markets (*ECM*) (see below).

Corporate finance is about building relationships with companies as much as it is about transactions. Before we describe the roles of the corporate financier in the above transactions, we need to place the corporate finance department in the context of an investment bank.

## CHINESE WALLS

Corporate financiers are said to work behind Chinese Walls – separating them from other members of the firm, in particular those who have daily contact with investors. The name, presumably, is taken from the Great Wall of China.

Chinese Walls are established arrangements in the form of procedures, systems, management and physical location which act as barriers within a firm to ensure that confidential information which is generated by one part of the firm or obtained from a client in one part of the firm (i.e., Corporate Finance) does not penetrate another part of the firm (i.e., Research, Sales and Trading).

They exist (or should do) in any integrated securities firm, investment bank, accounting firm or any other organisation where some members of the firm have access to and deal with information that could affect the share price of clients. Strengthening Chinese Walls became increasingly important in the aftermath of the 'Internet Bubble' of the late 1990s and early 2000s. Research analysts, particularly in the US, became highly involved in IPOs and further equity offerings, where they should not have done.

Corporate finance departments in large investment banks are almost always located on a separate floor than other departments. In some cases, at the largest banks, the corporate finance team may even reside in another building. At the very least, access is restricted in the corporate finance area to those who work there or escorted visitors who are signed in and out.

Chinese Walls provide a mechanism for firms to function as multi-disciplinary operations. Without Chinese Walls, a firm could not offer both corporate finance advice and research, sales and trading with clients. They work like porous membranes that allow information to flow only in one direction as illustrated in Figure 1.1.

Corporate financiers' work involves 'price-sensitive' information. Knowing that Company A plans to bid for Company B would send B's share price shooting up if the information found its way to the market. If a sales-

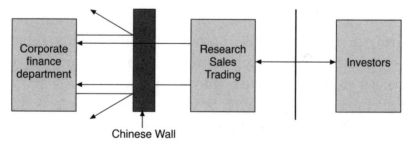

*Figure 1.1*   Information flow through the Chinese Wall – arrows represent the flow of information, and its direction.

man in the investment bank working on the bid discovered the potential bid as a result of weak Chinese Walls, he or she potentially could feed the information to selected clients who would benefit illegally from this inside information on announcement of the bid.

If Company C plans to raise funds through a new equity issue, the Chinese Wall should be maintained until announcement, as share prices typically drop on announcement of new issues. A party with inside information, gained from a leaky Chinese Wall, would be able to sell shares prior to the announcement of a new issue and buy them back at a lower price following the offering's announcement.

In order to advise clients, corporate financiers must receive information regarding the market, investors' attitudes, etc. from research analysts and salesmen who are in contact with investors. However, the confidential corporate information received by corporate financiers must not flow in the other direction as it could have an impact on the price of the shares.

# CORPORATE FINANCE ASSIGNMENTS

The following paragraphs contain summaries of the corporate finance role in major corporate transactions.

## Flotations/IPOs

The IPO of any company is one of the most important moments in its corporate life – it only happens once, and while companies can become skilled at acquisitions and divestitures, they do not get practice of IPOs. Thus, the role of the corporate financier in guiding companies and their management to market is crucial.

Many investment banks have specialist departments that sit alongside corporate finance – called Equity Capital Markets (ECM). ECM professionals specialise in the flotation of companies and any subsequent equity offerings. Throughout the book, I refer to 'corporate financiers'; in sections relating to equity new issues (Chapters 3–5), the reader should understand that a person in ECM would be doing the same job.

The corporate finance team co-ordinates the flotation process from start to finish. Figure 1.2 provides a schematic of the interested parties in a flotation. The

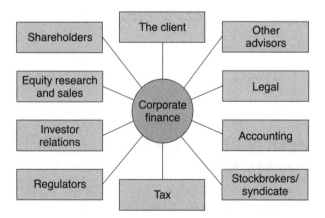

*Figure 1.2* Parties involved in flotations and M&A.

corporate financier keeps everything together: he or she is the main interface with the company, although solicitors, accountants and investor relations people also sit around the meeting table.

Chapters 3 and 4 provide a full description of the flotation process, from both the domestic and international perspective. The following paragraphs briefly summarise the corporate financier's role in these transactions.

The corporate finance team is usually the first appointed external advisor. It then aids the company in selecting the other advisors to work on the transaction. Corporate financiers provide advice on the capital structure, developing the investment story, appointing external directors, determining the timing of an issue and, generally, managing the project.

The team then co-ordinates the new issue timetable. From start to finish, the flotation process takes from 3 to 6 months, sometimes longer if there are particularly difficult corporate structuring issues to be resolved.

Corporate financiers deal with documentation (listing particulars, prospectuses, underwriting agreement) and the regulators. They are also responsible for the co-ordination of the different departments in their investment bank and members of the syndicate (i.e., equity research has been produced, the sales departments know the timetable and devote sufficient time to the new issue, etc.).

Finally, junior members of the corporate finance team are responsible for the organisation of the closing dinner; a gala affair for all the participants in the transaction that usually takes place a month or so after the shares have been trading on the Stock Exchange.

### Rights issues/Secondary offerings

Corporate financiers and their equity capital markets colleagues perform much the same role in rights issues and secondary offerings as they do in flotations. They co-ordinate the work of the other advisors, lead the preparation of documentation, advise the issuer or vendor on the pricing of shares and so on.

There is one complication, and it can be a large one. During a rights issue, the company's shares continue to trade in the stock market every day and the fluctuations in price can be large. The biggest disaster in secondary offerings was the offer of BP shares just before the Stock Market crash of 1987. Prior to the announcement of a sale of shares at 330 pence, BP's shares had been trading in the 345p–355p range. The Stock Market crash occurred after the offering was underwritten (at 330p per share), but before it closed. Following the crash, BP shares traded well below 300p each, resulting in significant losses to the underwriters and sub-underwriters.

# Mergers, acquisitions and divestitures

After flotation, a merger or acquisition is the most significant corporate event that most companies go through. Corporate financiers, acting alone or alongside strategy consultants, help senior management with planning for the future. They may recommend a divestiture, acquisition or joint venture, depending on the client's strategic, operational and financial criteria. Once the client has decided what course of action to pursue, corporate financiers help in the execution of the transaction.

Whatever the recommendation, the corporate finance team will co-ordinate all parties involved in the transaction. Figure 1.2 is also appropriate to describe the corporate finance role in mergers, acquisitions and divestitures.

### Acquisitions and mergers

If the client has determined that growth through acquisition or merger is its preferred strategy, the corporate finance team swings into action.

The corporate financier will conduct a search of domestic and international businesses that fit his client's criteria. In most instances, the client will know its industry well enough to identify the most likely targets without the assistance of an investment bank. Corporate financiers add value in analysing potential targets, as well as in broadening the search to international markets, if required.

Working with the client, corporate financiers evaluate potential candidates to determine a short-list based on potential fit and the receptiveness to an offer. The friendly welcome of an offer is vital. Only in the Anglo-Saxon economies are hostile takeover bids common and commonly successful. The vast majority of transactions are 'friendly', although the press given to hostile bids makes them seem to be more prevalent.

Once the client has agreed a short-list, the bankers analyse each target's business, competitive position and future prospects. Valuations on a stand-alone and merged entity basis (i.e., including potential synergies) are conducted.

Corporate financiers (the senior ones) can act as confidential intermediaries in approaching the potential vendor. Depending on the experience and inclination of his client, the corporate financier can take the lead in negotiations throughout the transaction. In any event, he will help to develop a bidding strategy and assist in structuring and negotiating terms and conditions.

In integrated securities houses, the corporate financier will bring in his colleagues in funding departments who can arrange financing (both short-term and permanent). Investment banks are increasingly providing loans to help complete deals; competing with banks.

From the agreement to negotiate exclusively with his client through closing, the corporate financier co-ordinates the activities of the lawyers, accountants and other advisors in managing the due diligence effort and the documentation required to support and close the deal.

Of course, not all transactions happen in such a structured manner. In some instances, an offer can be devised, proposed and accepted over the course of a frantic weekend. Such speedy transactions are usually in contested situations, where the client is second into the battle over a target which has great strategic importance.

## Divestitures

Organised sales of divisions, subsidiaries or businesses make up the majority of M&A transactions. Investment bankers are hired in order to maximise the value received by the vendor, minimise the length of the process and minimise the disruption caused to management of the business that is for sale. On the other side of the transaction, interested purchasers hire investment banks to aid in valuation, deal structuring and negotiation.

The first stage in an orderly divestiture is to determine the most likely purchaser(s). To add value at this stage, the corporate finance team should decide on a short-list of the most likely purchasers based on business fit and the strategic rationale for the acquisition. Private equity houses are now included as potential purchasers in most transactions, as are international businesses.

At the same time as the team is assembling a list of potential bidders, others will conduct a valuation to determine the worth of the business. The valuation helps the vendor in deciding whether an offer should be accepted or not.

Corporate financiers also recommend whether a negotiated transaction (with only a small number of potential bidders invited to take part) or an auction should be held. The auction process best serves larger businesses that are likely to elicit a high degree of interest. The extra work should result in a higher sale price.

Next, the corporate finance team prepares a confidential information memorandum that describes the operations of the business, its markets and prospects, contains historical financial results and often includes management's forecasts for the next year.

Letters are sent to prospective purchasers, followed by telephone calls from corporate financiers attempting to determine their interest. Those who are interested receive a copy of the information memorandum.

In an auction, prospective buyers are given several weeks to submit an initial bid based on the information contained in the memorandum. Once the preliminary, non-binding 'expressions of interest' are submitted, the corporate financiers assist the vendor in determining the short-list of potential purchasers. Bidders on the short-list then have access to a 'data room', which has more information than contained in the information memorandum and site visits, if appropriate. Data rooms, which were once an actual room with reams of corporate information, now are often 'virtual'. PDF files, with confidential information are posted on a secure Internet site, accessible to potential bidders via a password.

Throughout the process, corporate financiers manage

the distribution of information, contact with management and aim to maintain competitive tensions between/among potential bidders.

When the final bids are submitted, corporate financiers aid in evaluation of the offers and assist in negotiations over the terms and conditions until the sale is complete.

## Leveraged buyouts and management buyouts

Corporate financiers advise management groups on structuring, arranging financing and implementing buyouts of divisions, privately held businesses and public to private transactions (where a public company is purchased and delisted from the Stock Exchange).

# FINANCIAL ADVICE

A good corporate financier monitors his clients' share price and reputation among investors. When the market persistently undervalues a company, the corporate financier provides advice regarding actions his client might take. These actions might include disposal of certain divisions, a 'carve-out' (IPO of part of a subsidiary) or increasing the gearing of the balance sheet through share buybacks or special dividends.

Corporate financiers also provide fairness opinions to boards of directors. This typically involves the preparation of an independent valuation of potential acquisitions, divestitures or restructuring proposals. The opinion assures directors that the proposed transaction is fair, from a financial perspective, to all shareholders.

In the UK, all quoted companies must have a named financial advisor. The named advisor provides continuing advice in return for an annual retainer. The advisor also tends to be the investment bank that executes the majority of a client's transactions. However, companies are not bound to use their advisor on all or any transaction. Many companies will reward other investment banks with a leading role if the bank provides compelling ideas. Table 1.1 lists the top financial advisors as of mid-2005.

*Table 1.1*   Leading UK corporate finance advisors (by number of LSR clients).

| Rank | Advisor | Number |
|------|---------|--------|
| 1 | UBS Investment Bank | 117.0 |
| 2 | Seymour Pierce | 86.0 |
| 3 | Dresdner Kleinwort Wasserstein | 79.5 |
| 4 | KBC Peel Hunt | 76.0 |
| 5 | Brewer Dolphin Securities | 70.0 |
| 6 | Panmure Gordon & Co. | 68.0 |
| 7 | Evolution Securities | 67.5 |
| 8 | NM Rothschild | 64.5 |
| 9 | Collins Stewart | 55.5 |
| 10 | Teather & Greenwood | 47.5 |

*Note:* An advisor is awarded 0.5 if it shares a client with another advisor.

# CAREERS IN
# CORPORATE FINANCE

Corporate financiers will tell you that it takes a rare combination of attributes to be successful in their field. But they would, wouldn't they? According to established bankers, a corporate finance professional has the cunning of a snake, the stamina of a camel, the creativity of a chameleon, the memory of an elephant, the work ethic of a beaver, the negotiating finesse of a mouse sharing a bed with an elephant and so on.

To join the corporate finance zoo is not easy. Applications exceed the number of positions by multiples. The two main entry points are as executives/analysts and managers/associates. To get these sought-after positions investment banks universally demand:

- academic excellence;
- ability to work in teams;
- ability to work under pressure;
- quantitative skills;
- verbal and written communication strength.

The main entry points into corporate finance are as a graduate, following the completion of an accountancy designation, or following an MBA.

Box 1.1 gives excerpts from some job advertisements for the skills required.

*Box 1.1*   Excerpts from corporate finance job advertisements.

**1. Corporate Finance Executive**

Early responsibility is encouraged in an entrepreneurial team working closely with banks and insurance companies throughout Europe. Participate in both deal origination and execution including primary and secondary equity, M&A, advisory, and hybrid capital and debt.

Candidates should have financial institutions' experience gained either in investment banking, a 'Big 5' firm of chartered accountants or a leading law firm.

**2. Corporate Finance Associates and Analysts**

Will be involved in all aspects of analysis and presentations relating to mergers, acquisitions, divestitures, restructuring, leveraged buyouts and general corporate finance advice. Will participate in structuring and negotiating transactions and marketing.

Associates should have at least 3 years' experience in another leading investment bank. Analysts should be recently qualified ACAs or MBAs with relevant experience.

**3. Associate**

Associate to join team of leading investment bankers; considerable client contact and responsibility. Rapid career development possible.

ACA qualified with minumum 1 year's corporate finance transaction experience, or graduate with 2–3 years' experience in investment banking, M&A experience preferred. English mandatory, one other European language advantageous. Client-facing, results driven and ambitious.

**4. Manager/Associate Director**

The vacancy is for an established corporate financier with Yellow and Blue Book experience in transaction execution and an ability to originate at a senior level.

This role will attract a 'hands-on' marketeer wishing to be closer to the decision process and the client in a flexible, more entrepreneurial environment with a young culture.

Table 1.2 sets out illustrative job titles within a corporate finance department of a UK and a US investment bank. The paragraphs following the table provide more detail of the actual responsibilities held by the corporate financier at each level.

*Table 1.2*  Typical career progression of a corporate financier.

| Years of experience | Title(s) |
|---|---|
| 0–2 | Executive/Analyst |
| 3–4 | Manager/Associate |
| 5–8 | Assistant Director, Associate Director, Vice President |
| 8+ | Director |
| Too many | Managing Director |

Banks try to fill corporate finance with people who have the attention to detail, quantitative skills and stamina to successfully gather information, conduct valuations and carry out other tasks during the early years of their career. After being in the bank for 4 to 6 years, the most important skills gradually change, ultimately becoming the ability to manage existing clients and attract new ones.

The above is not meant to be a definitive list of titles. Banks are different; some have Assistant Managers, others both Assistant and Associate Directors. Titles change. Many organisations suffer from 'title inflation', a disease that occurs when too many big egos clash with a bonus pool that is too small.

Executives and Analysts are typically hired for corporate finance positions on completion of a degree. A small percentage may join a bank as an executive after a short stint at another job. Most larger banks have comprehensive induction/training programmes to ensure that all their employees start working life on an even footing. The role of the Executive/Analyst is to collect information, prepare valuations, keep notes of meetings, and aid in the drafting and proof-reading of prospectuses and takeover circulars. The days are long, the pressure high.

American investment banks have a tradition of chucking out all their analysts at the end of 2 years. The traditional analyst will then go to business school to get an MBA in the hopes of returning to the bank as an Associate; the sane ones go to Hawaii and take up surfing.

Managers and Associates are Executives who have put in around 3 years of hard graft. In addition, there is a large intake of recently qualified accountants at this level. In American banks, Associates arrive with MBAs. The Associate's job is similar to that of the Executive's, except there is more. Most Associates and Managers are assigned to industry teams, where they reside for 3 to 4 years.

The Corporate Finance role may be defined as one of project management. Mid-ranking corporate financiers, Associate Directors and Vice Presidents are expected to keep two, three or even four deals on the go at any one time (now that the Blackberry allows him to be in contact 24/7). At this level the job entails: making sure that the lawyers draft the documentation, accountants prepare financial statements and conduct due diligence, ensure that the PR team gains favourable press coverage and all the while 'holding the client's hand'. At this stage, the corporate financier is also spending more time marketing the firm's capabilities. (He's also probably questioning his sanity for staying in the business so long, but big mortgages and school fees keep the mind concentrated). After approximately 4 years in this role, the corporate financier can be expecting his next promotion.

The smart, some might say Machiavellian, corporate financier will make a habit of socialising and developing relationships with company managers who are 5 to 10 years older. Assuming that some of these friends and acquaintances are competent, they should be reaching senior corporate positions as the corporate financier becomes a director/managing director. These relationships should then bear fruit. A lucky corporate financier is one who has older siblings who are able to make appropriate introductions.

Directors and Managing Directors are generally responsible for client acquisition and retention. They go to the important meetings where decisions are taken, but they leave the day-to-day running of transactions to the people at the level below.

There are few corporate financiers who remain in the City after the age of 50 or so. Most switch to less pressurised jobs at client corporations, while a lucky few are able to retire at an early age in order to take up organic farming or purchase a vineyard.

# ORGANISATION OF THIS BOOK

This book has two parts. The first introduces the various types of transactions in which a corporate financier may become involved. It commences with an overview that presents the various forms of capital that a company may use in financing its operations or growth. Short- and long-term debt securities, ordinary and preference shares, and convertibles are described and their attributes listed. Those who have a grounding in finance or accounting can skim Chapter 2 or skip it entirely. The remainder of the book concentrates on ordinary shares, particularly the process by which companies issue new ordinary shares, and the purchase or sale of shares in an M&A transaction.

Chapters 3, 4 and 5 relate to equity fundraising – i.e., IPOs and further equity offerings. These chapters describe the process of the offerings, the documentation required, and how the marketing and sale of new shares is undertaken. Numerous examples are used to illustrate the transactions.

Chapters 6 and 7 look at M&A and Management Buy Outs. The reasons that a company might undertake an acquisition or divestiture are examined as are the existence of 'merger waves'. The regulatory aspects of public market transactions are presented.

Part II, which is the shorter of the two, covers some of the basics of valuation techniques that a corporate finance practitioner needs to have in his 'toolbox' in order to provide good advice to clients.

Chapter 8 describes the two main methods of corporate valuation that are in use today: comparable valuations and Discounted Cash Flows (DCF). A junior corporate financier can expect to spend much of his first 5 years putting together valuations as described in this chapter. Chapter 9 introduces some of the most common methods for determining the discount rate to be used in a DCF valuation. It also makes use of worked examples that should help the reader understand how the complex concepts are applied. The book concludes with a chapter on economic profit, more often referred to as shareholder value added. The ability to calculate a client's economic profit (or loss) will help the corporate financier to determine whether the client is creating value for its shareholders. If it is not, it may be possible that a corporate advisory assignment is in order.

# Part

# I

............................................

# CORPORATE
# FINANCE
# TRANSACTIONS

# Chapter

# 2

........................................

# SOURCES OF CAPITAL

Corporate finance at its most fundamental level is about how companies raise capital to run their businesses. Corporate financiers must understand the various sources of corporate funding and how they are combined to achieve an optimal capital structure.

The corporate financier advises on when and how to issue securities, at what price securities should be issued and, in some instances, how to repurchase securities. To do so, s/he must be familiar with the basic funding sources and know where to turn for assistance when considering more complex forms of finance. This chapter provides some detail on the characteristics of the main financial instruments available to companies.

During a company's life, its reliance on different forms of capital will change as illustrated in Figure 2.1.

The timing of the use of certain forms of finance will vary and not all companies will make use of each form of

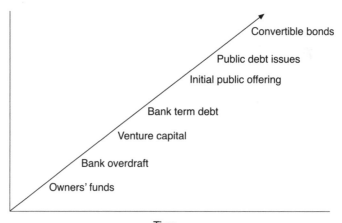

*Figure 2.1*   Financing life cycle.

capital. However, as you can see from the figure, there are two main forms of capital: debt and equity. The remainder of this chapter describes the primary forms of debt and equity that are available to UK corporations.

A good rule of thumb to keep in mind is that long-term assets such as plant and equipment should be financed with long-term liabilities (long-term debt or equity). Short-term assets such as stocks (inventory) or debtors (accounts receivable) generally can be financed with short-term liabilities.

# DEBT SECURITIES

Debt securities generally pay a periodic return to investors (interest payments, also referred to as the *coupon*) and return the initial investment to the holder on a predetermined date ('maturity'). Payment of interest and repayment of principal on debt securities are legal obligations of the issuer. Debt can be issued to the public ('debt securities') or raised from banks and other financial institutions ('bank loans'). Firms can issue either long-term or short-term debt. Short-term debt is defined as debt with a maturity of less than 1 year. The public market for short-term debt securities is called the *money market*. A short primer on bond valuation is included in Chapter 8 for readers who require it.

## Money market securities

Money market securities are tradable securities with a maturity of less than 1 year. Governments, banks and other financial institutions, and corporations issue money market securities. Corporations also invest in the money markets when they have excess cash. The largest money market in most countries is that of government-issued *Treasury Bills* (*T-bills*). All other money market securities are priced in relation to T-bills. The UK Government issues T-bills with 3- and 6-month maturities.

The main corporate money market instrument is *Commercial Paper* (*CP*). CP is a negotiable (i.e., it trades in the secondary market) promissory note. CP has a maturity (set on the issue date) of between 1 day and 1 year (note that American CP has a maturity of between 1 and 270 days). It is issued by large corporations on an unsecured basis. This means that companies simply promise to repay the purchasers of CP. If there is a default, CP holders do not have recourse to specified assets of the company, as would a mortgage lender if you stopped making payments on your house. CP issued in the Euro-markets is known as *EuroCommercial Paper* (*ECP*).

Both CP and ECP are the preserve of large corporations. Companies issue CP because the rate of interest paid is normally lower than that on bank overdrafts or loans. Issues can be arranged at very short notice and tailored to the exact funding requirements of the issuer.

*Bankers' Acceptances* (*BAs*) are tradable short-term corporate promissory notes that have been guaranteed ('accepted') for payment by a bank. BAs are issued by smaller companies or companies whose credit ratings don't allow them access to the CP market.

# Long-term debt

Debt with maturity greater than 1 year is also issued by governments, financial institutions and corporations. This debt is commonly referred to as the *bond/fixed income/fixed interest market* and comprises the largest segment of the capital markets. Fixed rate debt is the most common form of long-term debt: the coupon (interest payment) is set at the time of issue and continues at that level until maturity.

Longer term government securities in the UK are referred to as Gilts while long-term US government securities are Treasury Bonds. They are issued at par (£100 face value) and pay interest twice annually. The prices of bonds fluctuate with prevailing interest rates: rising as interest rates decline, falling as interest rates rise. Corporate bonds follow the same fluctuations and are priced in relation to Government Bonds.

Companies and financial institutions also issue long-term debt to finance capital investment and operations, known commonly as *bonds, notes* or *debentures*. The interest rate payable by these institutions varies based on the credit risk and maturity of the bonds. The interest rate will always be higher than that payable on government bonds issued in the same currency with the same maturity. This is known as the 'spread'. The spread over government bonds typically increases as maturity

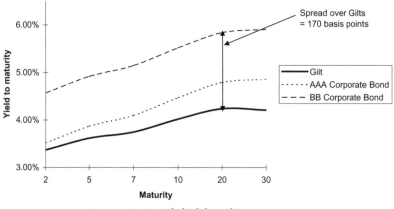

*Figure 2.2*   Global bond new issues.

increases or credit quality declines (as illustrated in Figure 2.2).

By far the largest corporate bond market is the US with $4,129 billion nominal value outstanding at year end 1999. The advent of the euro has led to a rapid increase

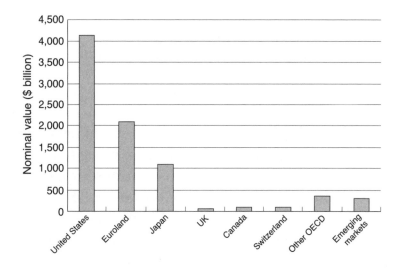

*Figure 2.3*   Bonds outstanding by country of issuer.

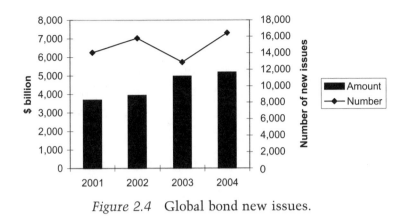

*Figure 2.4* Global bond new issues.

in issues by European corporations. At the end of 1999, there were $2,110.9 billion (nominal amount) of bonds outstanding issued by companies in 'Euroland'.

Global new issues of bonds ebb and flow with general economic conditions and interest rate expectations. Even in relatively slow years, new issues of bonds top $4 trillion. Yes, trillion (see Figure 2.4). While corporate financiers typically do not get involved in debt issues for their clients, they may make recommendations about general capital structure and market conditions that lead clients to a new issue.

# Floating rate notes

Floating rate notes have coupons or interest payments that vary with market conditions. The coupon rate is typically reset every three or six months. The most common reference rate for floating rate securities is the *London Inter-Bank Offer Rate (LIBOR)*. LIBOR is the rate of interest that major banks charge each other and is set every day for a variety of currencies. Banks set rates for US dollar LIBOR, Sterling LIBOR and Euro LIBOR (or *EURIBOR*) among many others. Since the coupon is reset frequently, the price of a floating rate note is not as volatile as that of a fixed interest bond.

### Illustration of different forms of debt finance

Box 2.1 is an excerpt from the Annual Report and Accounts published by British Telecommunications plc (*BT*) for the year ended 31 March 2005. It shows how large corporations issue debt in different maturities and in different currencies.

# EQUITY
## Preference shares

Preference shares (preferred shares) are shares which have defined rights to the profits and distributions of capital of a firm. These rights are usually limited to a specified dividend amount, which must be paid prior to the payment of dividends to ordinary shareholders. Common characteristics of preference shares include:

- A fixed dividend which is usually set as a percentage of the nominal or par value of the share (e.g., a preference share with a par value of 100p might carry an 8.0% dividend or 8p per share payable annually).
- Restricted voting rights. Preference shares typically have no voting rights unless the payment of dividends is in arrears.

*Box 2.1* BT balance sheet 31 March 2005 – loans and other borrowings.

| | 2005 £m | 2004 £m |
|---|---|---|
| US dollar 8.875% notes 2030 (min. 8.625%) | 1,604 | 1,606 |
| 5.75% bonds 2028 | 596 | 596 |
| 3.5% index-linked notes 2025 | 278 | 270 |
| 8.625% bonds 2020 | 297 | 297 |
| 7.75% notes 2016 (min. 7.5%) | 692 | 691 |
| Euro 7.125% notes 2011 (min. 6.875%) | 755 | 734 |
| US dollar 8.375% notes 2010 (min. 8.125%) | 1,754 | 1,795 |
| US dollar 8.765% bonds 2009 | 123 | 123 |
| Euro 11.875% senior notes 2009 | — | 3 |
| US dollar convertible 2008 (0.75%) | 88 | 97 |
| US dollar 7% notes 2007 | 573 | 596 |
| 12.25% bonds 2006 | 229 | 229 |
| 7.375% notes 2006 (min. 7.125%) | 399 | 398 |
| Euro 6.375% notes 2006 (min. 6.125%) | 1,923 | 1,861 |
| US dollar 7.875% notes 2005 (min. 7.624%) | 1,861 | 1,902 |
| US dollar 6.75% bonds 2004 | — | 597 |
| | | |
| Total listed bonds, debentures and notes | £11,172 | £11,875 |
| | | |
| Lease finance | 993 | 1,099 |
| Bank loans due 2007–2009 (average effective interest rate 9.7%) | 240 | 480 |
| Floating rate note 2005–2009 (average effective interest rate 3.8%) | 90 | 101 |
| Floating rate loan 2006 (average effective interest rate 5.6%) | 92 | 140 |
| Bank overdrafts and other short-term borrowing | 2 | 2 |
| | | |
| Total loans and other borrowings | £12,589 | £13,697 |

(cont.)

**Commentary:**

BT presents its long-term debt first, in chronological order, with issues with the longest maturity at the top. Here we can see that the longest maturity bond expires in 2030, 25 years from the date of the annual report, while one issue outstanding at the end of the 2004 fiscal year matured during the 2005 financial year (US dollar 6.75% bonds).

The company has issued debt in US dollars and euros as well as sterling. The company relies primarily on fixed rate debt, with only £320 in floating rate debt outstanding (both notes and bank loans).

- Priority in winding up. Preference shareholders will receive the par value of their shares before ordinary shareholders. Both types of shareholders rank behind all debt holders.

Dividends on preference shares are often cumulative – i.e., any arrears in the payment of preference shares must be caught up before ordinary share dividends may be resumed. Non-cumulative shares are the opposite of cumulative. If a company misses a dividend payment on a non-cumulative preference share, it is not required to make up the dividend.

# Ordinary shares

Investors who hold the ordinary shares of a corporation (common stock in the US) are the owners of the company. They have the right to share in the success and failure of the business indefinitely. In most countries, ordinary shareholders of publicly listed companies have the following common rights:

- a share in the profit of the business through the payment of dividends;
- voting privileges at annual general meetings to elect the board of directors;
- limited liability in the event that the company goes into liquidation;
- last claim on the assets of a company that goes into liquidation;
- to receive information in the form of an annual report including financial statements.

Ordinary shareholders receive a return through dividend payments as and when declared by the directors. Shareholders also anticipate returns through capital appreciation of the share price. Theoretically, the return on ordinary shares is unlimited and, occasionally, some companies do provide returns of over 1,000% in 1 year. Those that do, frequently give back 50% or more of their inflated value in the following year.

Occasionally, different voting rights will be attached to ordinary shares. The most common are non-voting shares and multiple voting shares. Non-voting shares are issued typically by parties who wish to raise funds in the capital markets, but do not want to give up control of the company. Differential voting rights leads to differential valuations being ascribed to the shares. Voting or multiple voting shares will be worth more than non-voting or subordinate voting shares.

# HYBRIDS (CONVERTIBLE SECURITIES)

Hybrid securities contain elements of both equity and debt. The most common hybrid in the UK is the convertible bond (sometimes referred to as a 'convertible debenture'). Less popular are convertible preference shares. In this section, convertible bonds are discussed, but most of the principles apply to convertible preference shares as well.

Global issuance of convertible bonds depends on general economic conditions and interest rate expectations like the straight bond market. However, equity market expectations also factor into the decision the issuance of a convertible. Issuers are often attracted to convertible bonds because they are viewed as the issue of deferred equity or equity at a higher price than today. Figure 2.5 illustrates recent convertible bond new issuance.

A convertible bond pays interest (convertible preference shares issue dividends) like a straight bond but, additionally, gives the investor the option to 'convert' the bond into a specified number of shares of the company at some date in the future. The conversion price is set at the time of issue and is typically above the share price at the time of issue. The difference is called the *conversion premium*. The right to convert the bonds into shares cannot be separated from the bond itself. In order to exercise her right to purchase the shares, an investor must surrender the convertible bond to the trustee

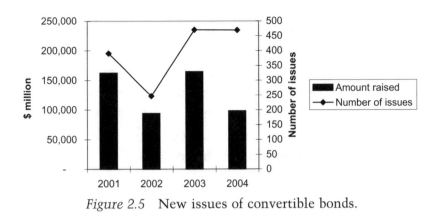

*Figure 2.5*   New issues of convertible bonds.

who will deliver the specified number of shares to the investor.

The interest rate paid on a convertible is lower than that on a straight bond issued by the company with the same maturity because the option to convert has a value for which investors are willing to pay. Note that the coupon on BT's US dollar convertible bond due in 2008 is a mere 0.75%, compared with a full 7.00% on its US dollar straight bond due in 2007.

The exchange feature of a convertible bond enables the holder to convert the par amount of the bond for ordinary shares at a specified price or 'conversion ratio'. The conversion ratio is set according to prevailing market conditions when the issue is launched. For example, a conversion ratio might give the holder the right to convert €100 par amount of the convertible bonds of Hightower Corporation into its common shares at €20 per share. This conversion ratio would be said to be 5:1 (i.e., the investor would receive five ordinary shares for each €100 par value bond on conversion).

The share price affects the value of a convertible substantially. Continuing with the example, if the shares of Hightower were trading at €10, and the convertible was trading at €100, there would be no economic reason for an investor to convert the bonds. For €100 par amount of the bond the investor would only get five shares of Hightower with a market value of €50.

But, why might the convertible be trading at €100 in this hypothetical case? The answer is that the yield of the bond justifies this price. For example, if the normal bonds of Hightower were trading at 10% yields and the yield of the convertible was 10%, bond investors would buy the convertible bond (in the hopes of the share price increasing) which would support its price. A convertible bond with an 'exercise price' far higher than the market price of the stock is called a 'busted convertible' and generally trades at its bond value.

When the share price attached to the bond is sufficiently high or 'in the money', the convertible begins to trade more like an equity. If the exercise price is much lower than the market price of the common shares, the holder of the convertible can convert into the stock attractively. If the exercise price is €20 and the stock is trading at €50, the holder can get five shares that have a market value of €250 for €100 par amount. This would force the price of the convertible above the bond value and its market price should be above €250 as convertibles usually have a higher yield than ordinary shares' dividends.

# Chapter

# 3

.........................................

# FLOTATIONS/ INITIAL PUBLIC OFFERINGS

A flotation is the initial sale of a company's shares to the public and the listing of the shares on a stock exchange. Flotations are also called Initial Public Offerings (*IPOs*). The process of flotation is long and arduous, involves significant time commitments from the company's management and advisors (investment bankers, stock brokers and solicitors amongst others) and is not cheap. So why do companies float? Put simply, to raise cash; either for the company itself (a primary offering) or for the existing shareholders (a secondary offering).

This chapter begins by describing the rationale behind flotations. An overview of the offering process is followed by more detailed discussions of the legal and documentary requirements and the process of marketing, syndication and sales.

## PRIMARY OFFERINGS

Companies which are raising capital by creating and selling new shares may do so for many reasons:

- to raise cash in order to expand the business of the company;
- reduce the debt levels (gearing) of the company;
- obtain access to alternative sources of finance;
- enhance its image and publicity;
- motivate and retain management and employees through share ownership and options;
- exploit a perceived mis-pricing by investors.

Flotation is often seen as the final step in the financial development of a company. On establishment, it is the savings of their founders that typically finances companies. As the company grows, the founders may borrow or seek investment from friends and family. If a company is growing rapidly, it may require additional equity capital, provided by a venture capitalist or institutional investors. At a certain level of development, long-term bank financing may be sought. Finally, the company goes to the public markets by flotation to finance the next stages of its growth. This was introduced in the financing life cycle chart in the previous chapter.

Many believe there is considerable prestige attached to managing and working for a publicly listed company. A quotation may bring marketing benefits, by making the company seem stronger and more substantial. Press coverage of public companies is typically greater than that of privately owned firms. Listing on an exchange allows employee shareholders to see the value of their holdings on a daily basis.

Another benefit ascribed to flotation is the ability to gain access to alternative sources of capital in the future. Quoted companies often are able to raise money for expansion more easily and at better rates than private companies of similar size. The public debt markets are more accessible to Stock Exchange quoted companies than to companies without a listing.

Although perceived mis-pricing (i.e., overpricing) by the markets is occasionally cited as a reason for flotation,

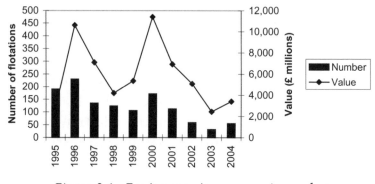

*Figure 3.1*   Equity new issues – main market.
Source: LSE – Primary Market Fact Sheet.

this is usually a matter of timing. Hot, new issue markets, such as the surge of biotechnology IPOs during the early 1980s or Internet stocks during the late 1990s may influence a company's management to go public at an earlier date than originally planned. Likewise, if the shareholders wish to sell, they may undertake a public offering rather than a trade sale if public markets are willing to pay a higher price than industry purchasers.

### Secondary offerings

In this section, secondary offerings refer to offerings where existing shareholders sell shares in the company, pocketing the proceeds. Secondary offerings are often combined with primary offerings where the company keeps the cash from the IPO.

There are numerous reasons why existing shareholders may wish to sell part or all of their shareholding through flotation. Occasionally, this type of offering is referred to as a 'secondary offering', which refers to the fact that no new shares are sold and that the company receives no cash. Some of the reasons follow:

- succession planning;
- diversification of holdings;
- venture capitalists and private investors seeking an 'exit' from their investment;
- equity carve-outs;
- privatisations of state-owned enterprises.

Succession is the cause of a number of flotations of small- and medium-sized companies. If younger members of the owner's family have no interest in, or aptitude for, the business, the owner may sell the company. Flotations resulting from succession factors increased during the late 1990s, particularly in continental Europe. Flotations may also occur when the second or third generation of family owners cannot get along. This was reputed to be a factor leading to the 1995 flotation of the Gucci fashion business.

The shareholders may have financial needs that can only be met by flotation. For example, the owner may decide that he no longer wishes to have his entire wealth bound up in the company. By selling a portion, the owner is able to diversify his investments. This was the reason for the large (£2 billion plus) offering of Wellcome plc shares in 1992. The Wellcome Trust, which owned 74% of the company prior to the offer, sold Wellcome plc shares and used the funds raised to diversify its holdings. The diversified holdings produced a higher income than Wellcome dividends, which the Trust used to increase its donations to medical research.

Equity carve-outs or spin-offs are a related type of offering. In an equity carve-out, the parent company sells a portion (usually between 20% and 49%) of a subsidiary company to the public. An equity carve-out can raise cash for either the subsidiary or the parent while control remains with the parent.

Research indicates that the announcement of an equity carve-out will increase the parent company's stock price by approximately 3%. The benefits of an equity carve-out include an increase in information to shareholders regarding the division and an increase in management accountability, focus and incentives. Investors believe that the subsidiary will perform better and, therefore, the value of the parent's investment will increase.

For example, Dixons, a UK retailer of electronic equipment, took advantage of the Internet bubble by successfully 'carving out' 20% of its holding in Freeserve, an Internet service provider in an August 1999 flotation.

Many companies are backed by development or venture capital firms at an early stage, or have undergone a management buy-out backed by Venture Capitalists (VCs). These financial investors typically will want to realise their investment ('exit') within 3 to 7 years. Flotation is often the optimal method of maximising proceeds. Compared with other companies that have conducted IPOs, VC-backed companies tend to be younger, have more equity in their capital structure, and generally attract higher quality investment banks and auditors to work on their transactions.

An example of a particularly fast 'exit' via flotation was the case of Collins Stewart, a UK stockbroker bought by management from Singer and Friedlander in April 2000. Collins Stewart's management, backed by CVC Capital, Bank of Scotland and Parallel Ventures, paid £122 million for the company. In October 2000, 6 months after the purchase closed, the business was floated with a value of £326 million (or 316p per share). By the end of the first day's trading the company's share price was 365p, a further increase of 15%.

During the 1980s and 1990s, privatisation offerings from governments, first in the UK and then around the world,

*Table 3.1*   Largest privatisations to 2000.

| Rank | Date | Company | Country | Amount ($m) |
| --- | --- | --- | --- | --- |
| 1 | Nov-99 | ENEL | Italy | 18,900 |
| 2 | Oct-98 | NTT DoCoMo | Japan | 18,000 |
| 3 | Feb-87 | NTT | Japan | 15,097 |
| 4 | Nov-96 | Deutsche Telekom | Germany | 13,330 |
| 5 | Nov-97 | Telstra | Australia | 10,530 |
| 6 | Dec-90 | Regional electricity companies | UK | 9,995 |
| 7 | Dec-89 | UK water authorities | UK | 8,679 |
| 8 | Dec-86 | British Gas | UK | 8,012 |
| 9 | Oct-93 | Japan Railroad East | Japan | 7,312 |
| 10 | Oct-97 | France Telecom | France | 7,080 |

accounted for some of the largest flotations recorded, including €18 billion raised by the Italian Treasury in the sale of 35% of its interest in Enel, the electricity generator and supplier, in October 1999. At the time, the Enel offering was the largest ever privatisation or equity offering in the world. While privatisations have slowed from their previous pace, they continue to produce some of the largest IPOs and follow-on offerings.

## Ancillary benefits of flotation

The flotation process forces a company's management to formulate and articulate a clear business strategy, often for the first time. This clearly should be beneficial to the future success of the business. Along similar lines, the anticipation of public ownership leads many companies into improving their management and financial structure. Fast-growing medium-sized companies often neglect the formal structures which will help them in their attempts to become large companies. The discipline of a public offering often helps in the creation of such structures.

## Disadvantages of flotation

Flotation does bring about some disadvantages, although each company will perceive them differently. There are the costs involved: both the direct costs (in time and money) of the flotation process as well as the costs of underpricing of the offering (see below) and the costs of increased disclosure to public shareholders (again, this is comprised of both time and money).

Other disadvantages include: the possibility that existing shareholders and/or management will lose control of the company and the increased pressure imposed on management because of scrutiny by shareholders.

# Methods of flotation

The British stock market is the third largest in the world by market capitalization, and has been so for a number of decades. The 'Official List' is the London Stock Exchange's (*LSE*) main market and home to corporate giants such as BPAmoco, GlaxoSmithKline and HSBC. It also hosts numerous much smaller companies such as Falcon Investments and World Trade Systems, with market capitalisations, as of April 2002, of £760,000 and £900,000, respectively.

Issuers have a choice between the LSE's main market and the Alternative Investment Market (*AIM*). AIM, which was established in 1995, is designed for smaller, more risky firms. The admission rules for companies joining AIM are less onerous than those for the LSE and ongoing regulation is lighter.

There are a number of different means by which a company can join the LSE or AIM. Depending on the issuer's requirements, these vary from a placing to institutional investors through global offerings to an offer for sale direct to the public. Indeed, on larger offerings, tranches of the offer may be dealt with by each method.

In an *Offer for Sale*, shares are offered direct to the public through advertisements in the national press. Offers for sale were most commonly seen in privatisations and where companies have a high profile or a large customer base. In an offer for sale, the allocation of shares is usually weighted towards the individual investor, while placings and global offerings favour the institutional investor. In an offer for sale, the price of shares is set prior to orders for shares being taken. Soundings are taken from institutional investors regarding pricing, prior to the share price being set and the offer being advertised in the press. Investors apply for shares by post or, more recently, over the Internet. Very few offers for sale occur these days.

When a *Placing* is used, the company's shares are sold to specific investors, typically institutions, but, on occasion, also to private individuals. The marketing of the issue is handled by the sponsor or broker who will decide on the target investors. The marketing is supported by the issue of a pathfinder prospectus (see below) and a series of presentations to individuals or groups of investors (the 'roadshow'). Individual (private) investors do not apply directly for shares as in an Offer, but must place an order through a stockbroker that is participating in the offering. Placings now dominate the UK market.

*Global offerings* are extensions of placings to target overseas investors. Such offerings can be achieved without necessarily listing shares on an overseas exchange. Box 3.1 is a copy of a newspaper advertisement announcing the Global Offering of Detica Group plc shares and its listing on the London Stock Exchange. Similar announcements are published when a placing occurs. A fuller discussion of international equity offerings follows in Chapter 4.

If the shares of a company are already widely held then it is possible to introduce those shares to the market in a process logically called an *Introduction*. This method is commonly seen where the company has no need for additional capital – e.g., on demutualisation of building societies.

## Suitability for listing

When the regulators of new issues – the UK Listing Authority (*UKLA*) in the UK and the Securities Exchange Commission (*SEC*) in the US – examine a company seeking to float and list on a stock exchange it has to determine whether a firm is suitable for listing. Typically, the regulator will examine the nature of the business – e.g., if the company is involved in illegal activities – as well as the following (which will be disclosed in the offering prospectus):

- experienced management and directors in place;
- conflicts of interest between the business and its shareholders;
- conflicts of interest with a director's private affairs;
- plans for the future and strategy;
- recently audited financial statements.

---

*Box 3.1*   Announcement of a new issue.

---

This notice is issued in compliance with the requirements of the Financial Services Authority (the FSA) and appears as a matter of record only. It does not constitute an offer or invitation to any person to subscribe for, or purchase, any securities of Detica Group plc in the United States or any other jurisdiction. The shares in Detica Group plc are not being registered under the US Securities Act of 1933, as amended (the Securities Act) and may not be offered or sold in the United States unless registered under the Securities Act or pursuant to an exemption from such registration. No public offer of shares in Detica Group plc will be made into the United States.

Application has been made to the FSA for the whole of the ordinary share capital of Detica Group plc, issued and to be issued, to be admitted to the Official List of the UK Listing Authority (admission) and to the London Stock Exchange plc (the London Stock Exchange) for such shares to be admitted to trading on the London Stock Exchange's market for listed securities. It is expected that admission of the ordinary shares of 2p each of Detica Group plc (the Shares) will become effective, and that dealings in the Shares will commence on 30 April 2002.

**Detica Group plc**
(incorporated and registered in England and Wales under the Companies Act 1985 with registered number 3328242)

Global offer of up to 9,050,389 ordinary shares of 2p each
(the Global Offer)
at a price expected to be between 440p and 510p
per ordinary share

Admission to the Official List of the UK Listing Authority and
to trading on the London Stock Exchange's market
for listed securities

Sponsored by UBS Warburg Ltd.

Expected share capital immediately following admission (assuming no exercise of the over-allotment option and an offer price of 475 pence, being the mid-point of the price range)

| Authorised | | | Issued and fully paid up | |
|---|---|---|---|---|
| Number | Nominal value | | Number | Nominal value |
| 35,000,000 | £700,000 | Ordinary shares of 2p each | 21,429,321 | £428,586 |

Detica Group plc is an established UK information technology (IT) services company that provides consultancy and systems implementation services primarily to two markets: the Customer Relationship Management (CRM) market and the UK national security market.

Listing particulars relating to the Global Offer, which have been approved by the FSA as required by the Listing Rules made under section 74 of the Financial Services and Markets Act 2000, were published on 8 April 2002. UBS Warburg Ltd is acting for Detica Group plc in connection with the Global Offer and no-one else and will not be responsible to anyone other than Detica Group plc for providing the protections afforded to clients of UBS Warburg Ltd or for providing advice in relation to the Global Offer. Copies of the Listing Particulars are available for inspection at the Document Viewing Facility of the Financial Services Authority, 25 North Colonnade, London E14 5HS and may be collected free of charge during normal business hours on any weekday (Saturdays, Sundays and public holidays excepted) from the date of this notice up to and including 23 April 2002 from:

| | | |
|---|---|---|
| Linklaters | Detica Group plc | UBS Warburg Ltd |
| One Silk Street | Surrey Research Park | 1 Finsbury Avenue |
| London | Guildford | London |
| EC2Y 8HQ | Surrey GU2 7YP | EC2M 2PP |

9 April 2002

Corporate finance advisors assist companies to prepare for flotations by making recommendations for non-executive directors, sorting out any internal conflicts of interest, aiding in the development of future strategy and putting management in contact with other professional advisors.

# THE OFFERING PROCESS

There are two main components to any flotation or IPO:

- documentation and regulation;
- marketing, syndication, distribution and pricing.

As markets have developed and become more sophisticated, the personnel involved in a new issue have become specialists. Now, only a few people at the lead investment bank involved in the transaction will have a full understanding of the status of both the legal and marketing aspects of the offering.

## Participants and roles

Preparing a company for flotation requires the involvement of a large number of players, each with a specific role to play. The leading participant, and generally the first advisor appointed, is a merchant bank or an investment bank. Occasionally, other professional advisors, such as stockbrokers or chartered accountants, can take this important role. The lead bank in a UK domestic IPO is called the *Sponsor*.

The sponsor develops the structure of the offering, helps to appoint other participants (solicitors, public and investor relations advisors, an American Depository Receipt – *ADR* – bank and registrars) co-ordinates all aspects of the issue, leads the drafting of documentation, organises the verification process and is generally the primary underwriter. The sponsor also formally backs the company's application for listing on the Stock Exchange.

The lead bank assembles a syndicate of banks and brokers to assist in the selling of the offering. Syndicate members are usually selected on the basis of their ability to distribute shares to investors and to provide company research following the offering. The size of the syndicate will depend on the size and structure of the offering and existing banking relationships which the issuer may have. In a 'traditional' UK offering, the appointed stock-broker handles communications with investors prior to the issue, assists in marketing the shares, arranges the sub-underwriting (see below) and is largely responsible for setting the issue price.

Two firms of solicitors work on new issues: the company's counsel and the solicitors who act for the banking syndicate, who are known as *Solicitors to the Issue*. The solicitors ensure that the documentation is accurate and draft the various legal agreements that are required (e.g., underwriting agreement). The Solicitors to the Issue have responsibility for legal due diligence during the flotation. This will include a verification process on the statements made in the prospectus and advising the sponsor on the statutory aspects of the issue.

The issuer's accountants – known as the *Reporting Accountants* – also have a role. They must ensure that the most recently audited financial statements are properly presented in the prospectus, conduct financial due diligence, conduct an investigation of the company and produce a 'long-form report'. In addition, the firm may be asked to produce a short-form report, as well as report on any profit forecast included in the listing particulars/ prospectus and examine the company's working capital requirements. If a US public offering is being considered, the Reporting Accountants must prepare the company's accounts according to the US Generally Accepted Accounting Principles (*US GAAP*).

It is common to hire public relations and investor relations consultants. These advisors co-ordinate any advertising to be undertaken, media relations and press conferences. Following the flotation, the investor relations advisor assists the company in the preparation of its interim and annual report and accounts, press releases related to the company's results and any other significant events. The investor relations advisor will also organise regular presentations to investors and research analysts who follow the company.

While the lawyers and bankers work on the documentation for the issue, the brokers, salesmen and syndicate members are preparing the market and selling the offering. This is all done within a fairly tight time frame with all-night sessions to meet certain deadlines not uncommon (see the outline flotation timetable in Figure 3.2). The remainder of this section deals with the two main aspects of the new issue – Regulation and Documentation, and Marketing, Syndication and Pricing.

Figure 3.2 provides a template for a flotation timetable. Not all offers will be completed in the time allotted, nor will other offers require all the time that is available under this timetable.

# Documentation and regulation

The main document delivered to investors in an equity offering is the *prospectus*. A prospectus contains information about the offering (price, number of shares on offer, subscription procedure), about the business of the company (industry, management and operations) and audited financial statements. The exact requirements for the contents of a prospectus vary from jurisdiction to jurisdiction.

In the UK, the main document that is submitted to the UKLA is referred to as the 'Listing Particulars'. These contain all the information contained in the prospectus as well as some additional information of a more technical nature that does not have a bearing on an investor's investment decision.

| Week | Pre-work | -12 | -11 | -10 | -9 | -8 | -7 | -6 | -5 | -4 | -3 | -2 | -1 | 0 | +1 | Beyond |
|---|---|---|---|---|---|---|---|---|---|---|---|---|---|---|---|---|
| Organisational and structural issues | ▓ | | | | | | | | | | | | | | | |
| Appoint advisors | ▓ | | | | | | | | | | | | | | | |
| Due diligence | | ▓ | ▓ | ▓ | ▓ | | | ▓ | ▓ | ▓ | ▓ | ▓ | ▓ | | | |
| Prospectus drafting | | ▓ | ▓ | ▓ | ▓ | ▓ | ▓ | ▓ | ▓ | ▓ | ▓ | ▓ | | | | |
| Regulatory review | | | | | | | | ▓ | ▓ | ▓ | ▓ | ▓ | | | | |
| Draft other documents | | | | | | ▓ | ▓ | ▓ | ▓ | ▓ | ▓ | ▓ | | | | |
| Syndicate presentation | | | | | | ░ | | | | | | | | | | |
| Pre-marketing | | | | | | | | | ░ | ░ | | | | | | |
| Research released | | | | | | | | | | ░ | | | | | | |
| Marketing | | | | | | | | | | | ░ | ░ | ░ | ░ | | |
| Roadshow | | | | | | | | | | | | ░ | ░ | ░ | | |
| Bookbuilding | | | | | | | | | | | | ░ | ░ | ░ | | |
| Final regulatory approval | | | | | | | | | | | | | ░ | ░ | | |
| Pricing | | | | | | | | | | | | | | ░ | | |
| Allocation | | | | | | | | | | | | | | ░ | | |
| Stabilisation | | | | | | | | | | | | | | | ■ | |
| End of lock-up | | | | | | | | | | | | | | | | ■ |

*Figure 3.2*  Outline flotation timetable. 'Pre-work' can begin anywhere from a few weeks to years before the start of this timetable – medium tinted areas are legal, regulatory and documentary; pale tinted areas reflect marketing activities; while dark tinted areas represent after-pricing issues.

# Due diligence and verification

Under securities legislation in most countries, the issuer assumes absolute responsibility that the information contained in the prospectus is accurate (see the declaration in Box 3.2 for the UK form). In addition, the managers of the offering have a separate responsibility to make a reasonable investigation to ensure the accuracy of the offering documents used in an IPO.

Thus, it is customary for the bankers and their counsel to conduct a *due diligence* examination of the company's business which might bear on the accuracy or fairness of any statement in the prospectus or might otherwise be of material interest to a potential purchaser. There is no prescribed routine or checklist for such an investigation; rather, its elements are usually discussed and agreed upon in advance by the bankers and the company, based on the nature of the particular offering.

In the UK, a process known as *verification* takes place. It is similar to due diligence in its thorough investigation of the company's operations and financial statements. However, it differs in that each statement in the prospectus is documented as a fact and the source of the information is collected and placed on file.

The completion of a thorough due diligence examination brings two benefits to the lead investment bank: first, it gives the bankers a deeper appreciation and understanding of the business of the company, allowing the bank to tailor the marketing story for investors. Second,

---

*Box 3.2   UK prospectus requirements*

---

**The persons responsible for listing particulars, the auditors and other advisors (banks, brokers and solicitors)**
This section includes the following declaration:

'The directors of [the issuer], whose names appear on page [ ], accept responsibility for the information contained in this document. To the best of the knowledge and belief of the directors (who have taken all reasonable care to ensure that such is the case) the information contained in this document is in accordance with the facts and does not omit anything likely to affect the import of such information.'

**The shares for which application is being made**
A description of the characteristics of the shares (e.g., voting rights), the number being offered, names of stock exchanges where listing is being sought are included.

**The issuer and its capital**
Name, registered office and head office of issuer. Description of share capital and any changes in prior 3 years. Controlling shareholders and any other holder of at least 3% of the capital.

**The group's activities**
Description of the business of the company, including breakdown of divisional turnover, number of employees, R&D main investments, etc.

**The issuer's assets and liabilities, financial position and profits and losses**
Three years of financial results in a comparable table (balance sheet, income statement and cash flow statement together with the notes to the accounts); 'working capital statement' (see below).

**The management**
Directors of the issuer with details of previous work; aggregate remuneration paid to directors.

**The recent development and prospects of the group**
General information on the trend of the group's business since the end of the financial year to which the last published annual accounts relate; this may include a profit forecast or estimate and the supporting grounds for the forecast or estimate (including the sponsor's statement).

**Working capital statement**
Companies listing in the UK must produce a working capital statement attesting to the directors' belief that the company will have sufficient working capital for 12 months following publication of the prospectus.

Although the company directors are legally liable for the statement, they will rely on a Working Capital Report produced by the company's accountants.

**Forecasts**
Forecasts are optional in UK prospectuses. Most companies include a forecast of earnings to the end of the fiscal year in which the prospectus is published. They will also include an anticipated dividend and calculate the anticipated dividend yield based on the new issue price and the anticipated dividend.

by conducting due diligence the managers of the offering are protected from lawsuits from disgruntled shareholders if the price drops dramatically in the market after the launch of the offering.

# Marketing, syndication and pricing

The marketing of equity new issues is a sophisticated process which involves three stages: pre-marketing to prepare investors for the issue; formal marketing once a preliminary prospectus has been printed; and, finally, pricing, allocation and distribution of the shares.

The initial phase is devoted to educating investors so that they understand the company and the industry in which it operates. Typically, a major research document is published by the brokers to the issue and distributed to investing institutions up to 8 weeks prior to the anticipated offering date. While the investors study the research report, the lead bank and investor relations consultants work with the company's management to prepare the management for the second phase of marketing – meeting the investors.

The second phase commences with the publication of a preliminary prospectus (referred to as a *pathfinder prospectus* in the UK). In most large offerings, the preliminary prospectus is published approximately 4 to 5 weeks before the price of the issue is set. The preliminary prospectus includes nearly all the necessary information required to make an investment decision, except the share price. Usually, the lead bank will indicate a price range at this time, so that investors have an idea of the valuation being contemplated.

After the preliminary prospectus has been published, company management commence presentations to institutional investors, known as a 'roadshow'. The programme includes a combination of one-on-one meetings with the most important institutions and breakfast, lunch and dinner presentations to selected groups of fund managers and analysts.

In a *Placing* or *Global Offering* (more about which in Chapter 4), during the last stages of the marketing period prior to pricing, institutional investors are canvassed by the banks and brokers involved, for their interest in purchasing shares. As the pricing date approaches, the indicated price range narrows. This allows the sponsors of the issue to more accurately set the price in light of investor demand. Some use sophisticated computer software to model demand at specific price points and use this to set an 'optimal issue price'.

Pricing a new issue is not an exact science, however. Most flotations are priced in the expectation that the shares will begin trading at approximately 10% above the issue price. In IPOs of highly risky companies – e.g., Internet and biotechnology businesses – the level of underpricing is greater. In offerings where existing shares are already trading in the market, the offering process attempts to price the new shares being offered slightly below the existing share price. This is discussed in Chapter 5 (on *secondary offerings*).

The third and final stage of the new issue marketing process is the allocation of shares to investors, once the price has been set and all orders placed. While the decision on price is fundamental to the success of the issue, the allocation policy has an important role, not only in the aftermarket, but also in the maintenance of a strong and stable shareholder base. Allocations are generally spread among three or four classes of investor: a small group of core investors, other long-term investors, private clients and, finally, short-term traders.

Short-term traders (or *stags*) purchase new issues in the hopes of selling the shares immediately for a small profit and provide immediate liquidity in the shares. It is important to control the allocation of shares to the 'stags' so as to ensure orderly trading during the first few days after issue.

If the offering is over-subscribed, the sponsor and brokers must determine how to allocate the shares. They have two options: to scale down allotments on a *pro rata* basis or make random allotments using a ballot. In a ballot, some or all of the applications may be 'put into a hat' and applications drawn at random to be granted part or all of the shares applied for. Applications not selected are unsuccessful and investors' money is returned.

The allocation of shares from a new issue is made by means of an allotment letter. This entitles the recipient to a specified number of shares, subject to payment.

## Underwriting

In an Offer for Sale the share price is set after negotiation between the bankers, brokers and the issuer. Once set, the issue is 'underwritten' and the formal selling period begins. Price setting in placings is similar to that in international offerings and is described in Chapter 4.

Underwriting guarantees the issuing company or selling shareholders the proceeds of the offering (less expenses). If the underwriters – usually, the lead bank(s) – are not able to sell the shares to investors (whether a result of mis-pricing, adverse market conditions or any other reason) they must purchase the shares not sold from the issuer at the issue price.

The underwriting period will vary, but it starts when the price is set (known as *Impact Day* in the UK) and continues to the close of the subscription period (between 1 and 3 weeks). If the issuer is seeking to attract individual investors, it must leave the subscription period open for a sufficient length of time for the investors to respond to the offer.

To spread risk, it is common for the lead bank to 'sub-underwrite' among a group of banks, brokers and investing institutions in order to spread the risk of failure. The sub-underwriting takes place immediately after the price has been set. Each sub-underwriter agrees to guarantee the sale of a small portion of the amount being raised, generally between 1 and 2%.

# Chapter

# 4

.......................................

# INTERNATIONAL
# EQUITY OFFERINGS

S ince the mid-1980s, international equity offerings (a new issue of shares offered in several markets simultaneously) have experienced explosive growth. Government privatisation programmes fuelled this growth by increasing interest in equity investment in both developed and emerging markets. As the market evolved, so did the procedures surrounding the launch of an international offering.

International equity offerings are a relatively new phenomenon (i.e., since the 1980s). Although companies have raised funds outside their own markets for decades (centuries even), the first co-ordinated, simultaneous offering of shares in a domestic market with a separate international tranche targeted at foreign investors occurred in 1983.

This chapter outlines the reasons companies go to the extra effort and expense to sell shares internationally, highlights the key documentation, and describes the marketing and distribution processes used by investment banks in international equity offerings.

# RATIONALE FOR INTERNATIONAL OFFERINGS

An issuer can sell shares exclusively to domestic investors or it may decide upon an international offering. The domestic offering is the route chosen for most smaller (i.e., under $100 million) flotations. It is generally cheaper and simpler to complete.

However, there are many reasons for an issuer to contemplate accessing international investors in its initial public offering. A broader shareholder base is likely to increase demand for its shares and, therefore, maximise the value of the offering. A company's international profile certainly will be increased by offering shares outside its home country which may benefit the company's business.

Another benefit (cited regularly in the late 1980s) was that international distribution of a company's shares was useful in merger and acquisition activity. The theory being that if a company's shares were well known outside its own market, it could use the shares as currency for international acquisitions. For example, Daimler Benz of Germany listed its shares on the New York Stock Exchange a few years before it acquired Chrysler Corporation. In addition, it was believed that widespread international shareholdings of a company's stock would reduce its vulnerability to hostile takeovers.

In certain industries, companies have found it beneficial to go to the international market because investors outside their domestic market value the securities more highly than do domestic investors. This may be because the international market has more experience of a certain industry, or because of temporary anomalies.

One example of this was the dual listing of many British cable television companies in London and on the NASDAQ market in the US in 1994 and 1995. Investors in America had much more experience of the cable TV industry than did those in Britain and were prepared to pay a higher price for the shares. Another example was the surge of international mining companies which listed on the Toronto Stock Exchange during the 1990s and 2000s, because companies perceived that the investors and advisors were more experienced and knowledgeable and would pay higher prices for mining company shares.

Other issuers have turned to international markets because their home market was too small to supply the funds required. This has occurred often in the Scandinavian markets and in the emerging markets of central and eastern Europe.

## International investors

While the above section outlines the corporate drivers for international offerings, there is increasing pull, or demand, from institutional investors. There are several reasons for this, including:

- More securities and industries to choose from.
- Greater returns – many emerging markets provide higher rates of return than do more mature markets and some markets may not be as efficient as others, allowing professional investors an advantage.
- Reduction of risk – not all national stock markets advance (or decline) at the same time. Therefore, international diversification may reduce risk in a portfolio context.

- Liquidity – some institutions demand significant liquidity in their portfolios which can only be met by investing in the largest global companies.

# Development of international equity offerings

International equity offerings received a significant boost in 1984 from the UK Government's privatisation of British Telecom (*BT*). Shares were offered in public offers in the UK, Canada and the US. BT shares were also distributed to investors in the rest of Europe and the Middle East. The Government took the decision to launch an international offering because it believed that the UK equity market was too small to absorb such a large issue without seriously affecting the price the Government would receive.

The offering was a huge success and the UK continued its privatisation programme through multi-tranche international offerings with the sale of British Gas, British Airways, British Petroleum, the ten water companies, the electricity industry and Railtrack.

The 1990s witnessed the emergence of US investors as one of the driving forces behind international offerings. This was caused by two factors: the reallocation of assets from domestic to international investments on the part of US institutional investors, and an easing of new issues regulation by the US securities regulators.

In 1990, it was estimated that US pension funds had approximately 3% of their total assets invested in

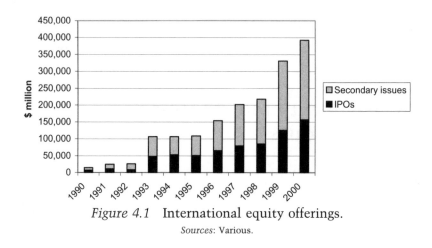

*Figure 4.1* International equity offerings.

*Sources*: Various.

non-US shares. By 1995 this figure had risen to approximately 8% and grew to 12% in 2001. In comparison, UK institutional investors typically hold approximately 25% of their portfolios in overseas equities and have done so for many years.

The growth of the market for international equity offerings is illustrated in Figure 4.1.

# Regulation and documentation

If an offering of shares is made to the public in the US, a registration statement must be filed with, and approved by, the *Securities Exchange Commission (SEC)*. The registration statement (Form F-1 for international companies) is similar to the UK's Listing Particulars, in that it contains a prospectus that is sent to potential investors as well as additional information for the regulators. The local market prospectus and US registration statement will have identical content if not identical form.

It is necessary to ensure that investors in all markets receive the same information.

SEC regulations require the registration statement to include a consolidated balance sheet, a 3-year consolidated income statement and a 3-year consolidated statement of cash flows, each certified by an independent accountant and prepared in accordance with US GAAP. This process can be very expensive and time consuming as companies comply with the financial disclosure requirements.

Compliance with US accounting rules can also throw up anomalies, such as when Daimler Benz listed its shares on the New York Stock Exchange. According to US GAAP, the company lost nearly $1 billion in the year prior to listing, but according to German accounting standards, it had been profitable.

A preliminary prospectus ('red herring') is circulated among prospective investors simultaneously with the SEC's review of the documentation. The review process typically takes from 4 to 6 weeks to complete. Once the SEC has approved any changes that have been required, the investment banks can sell the shares to investors.

Box 4.1 summarises the key parts of a US prospectus.

In most other jurisdictions, when shares are being offered in a foreign company to sophisticated institutional investors, separate prospectuses need not be produced, nor is the main prospectus reviewed by the regulators. In Japan, which was once a huge market for

*Box 4.1*   Key requirements of a US prospectus

**(1) Front cover**
Gives general information such as the issuer's name, type and amount of securities being offered and whether existing shareholders are selling any shares. If an IPO, it will state that there has been no public market up to now. It will also name the managers of the offering and the amount of their compensation and expenses of the issue.

**(2) Summary of the Offering**
Information regarding the company that is repeated elsewhere, details of the offering and expected timetable.

**(3) Key information**
Selected financial data, capitalization and indebtedness, and use of proceeds. This information is often included as part of the Summary and again immediately prior to Management Discussion and Analysis.

**(4) Company information**
Detailed disclosure of the company's history, business plan, organizational structure, operations and competition.

**(5) Management Discussion and Analysis**
Operating results, liquidity and capital resources, and trend information.

**(6) Directors and senior management**
Including details of their compensation, employees and share ownership.

**(7) Major shareholders and related party transactions**

**(8) The offer and listing**
Offer and listing details, plan of distribution, markets, selling shareholders, dilution and expenses of the issue.

**(9) Risk Factors or Investment Considerations**
Generally appears near the front of the prospectus. Each risk factor mentioned will also be disclosed and discussed in more detail in the rest of the prospectus.

**(10) Description of securities other than equity securities**
Debt securities, warrants and rights, American Depository Shares, etc.

**(11) Financial information**
Audited consolidated statements and notes to financial statements.

international shares, private placement rules allow the banks or brokers arranging the sale to approach up to 50 investors without requiring regulatory review. If the banks wish to approach more institutions, they must either apply for an exemption from the Ministry of Finance or file an offering document.

# Depository receipts

Many US investors participate in international offerings by purchasing Depository Receipts (*DRs*) issued by foreign (non-US) companies. DRs are a convenient mechanism for transferring ownership, receiving dividends and taking care of other routine transactions in foreign securities. Far from being a recent innovation, the first DRs were issued by JP Morgan in 1927 for a number of Scandinavian corporations.

There are two main types of depository receipts: *American Depository Receipts (ADRs)* and *Global Depository*

*Receipts (GDRs).* ADRs are quoted and traded in US dollars in the US markets (either on an exchange or over-the-counter). GDRs may be quoted in US dollars, but also in pounds sterling and occasionally in another currency. GDRs are often listed in London or Luxembourg. The principles surrounding the operation of each are the same.

DRs are issued by a 'depository bank' which holds the underlying shares in custody. The depository acts as a transfer agent for the DRs, distributes dividends in dollars (or sterling) and distributes corporate information, such as annual reports and accounts.

The advantages to issuers include the following: ability to access a broader shareholder base and increased liquidity outside the company's home market; enhanced ability to raise new capital in the US (with respect to ADRs) and internationally (with respect to GDRs). Academic research suggests that a company with an ADR listing can reduce its cost of equity by approximately 1% (see Chapter 9 for a discussion of cost of equity).

Companies that don't want to go to the expense and effort of a US public offering may elect to offer shares to institutional investors through a private placement.

The SEC's Rule 144a allows issuers to sell shares or ADRs to Qualified Institutional Investors (*QIBs*) which are large investing institutions. The SEC receives a copy of the prospectus used in a Rule 144a offering, but does not review or pass judgement on it. The introduction of

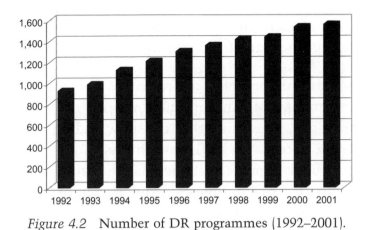

*Figure 4.2* Number of DR programmes (1992–2001).

Rule 144a in 1990 was the event that led US investors to increase their participation in international offerings.

With the growth in importance of US demand and the influence of US investment banks, the international equity market has adopted many American techniques and practices, particularly with respect to marketing and pricing new issues.

# Marketing, syndication and distribution

In international offerings, it is standard to assemble a group of banks (a 'syndicate') who each sell the securities being offered to ensure wide distribution of the shares. The participants in the syndicate are called *Managers*. Within each syndicate, there is a hierarchy, adapted from the Eurobond market: lead manager, co-lead manager, and co-manager. If there is more than one lead manager, it is customary to appoint one as the 'bookrunner' or global co-ordinator. There will be several managers in each geographic jurisdiction, depending on the size of the offering.

The bookrunner or global co-ordinator, is responsible for the documentation (in conjunction with the lawyers), due diligence, organising the roadshow and other tasks, just as the sponsor to a UK flotation is. It also controls the order book (hence the name), has the final say on the allocation of shares to investors and, therefore, is able to favour investors which place orders with it. There is fierce competition among investment banks to be the bookrunner on transactions.

From approximately 1993 to 2000, there was a tendency among issuers to appoint two or more investment banks as joint bookrunners, or co-global co-ordinators. Initially, a home-market investment bank was appointed in conjunction with a global investment bank. Since 2001, the number of global co-ordinators included in an offering has tended to decrease.

Co-lead, co-managers and managers do not participate in the preparation of the legal and documentation aspects of the offering. They are invited into the syndicate to add distribution by selling to as many potential investors as possible and to provide a research following for the company after the issue.

## Offer structure

An international offering is typically divided into tranches: the domestic tranche, where shares are sold to investors in the company's home market and an international tranche. The international tranche is occasionally further sub-divided depending on the offering.

In the early days of international equity offerings it was not uncommon to have up to a dozen separate international tranches, each devoted to a single country. Banks participating in the Italian tranche of an international offering, for example, could sell only to investors in Italy. Current practice is to limit the number of tranches in order to allow the global co-ordinator more flexibility in allocating shares to the regions where demand is greatest.

Many Initial Public Offering (IPOs) and follow-on offerings employ a single global syndicate, where there are no separate tranches and the senior banks in the syndicate sell shares in whatever market they find demand (subject to local restrictions). This approach was first used in the third BT offering in 1993. Many bankers believe that global syndicates work better if the securities being sold have already been listed and have a wide following.

# Price setting, underwriting and bookbuilding

International offerings exclude a sub-underwriting group. International practice, adopted from the US, has been to undertake substantial pre-marketing or 'bookbuilding' prior to pricing. During the marketing period, investors indicate their demand for shares at different price levels: the order 'book'. Subsequently, the bookrunner, in discussion with the issuer, may vary the size of the issue or its price, or both, in an attempt to satisfy the level of indicated demand. The bookrunner then sets the price of the issue to maximise proceeds, while ensuring that there is unsatisfied demand, so that investors will purchase shares in the market following the offering.

In the US market when the issue is priced, underwriting commitments are made similarly to European practice. Typically, US issues are priced after the stock exchanges have closed for the day. Allocation of shares among investors commences that evening and continues the following morning prior to the opening of the exchanges. Once allocation to investors has been made, the investment bank's underwriting commitment expires. Thus, the underwriters are not exposed to fluctuations in the market – the underwriting period (i.e., the length of time for which the underwriters are at risk) rarely lasts 24 hours.

Increasingly, international issuers are opting to follow this offering procedure: set the price and make allocations on Sunday or when the home market has closed and commence trading the following morning. If there has been a public offering in the US, and that has been a major component of the issue, often trading in a European offering will not begin until New York opens (i.e., 2.30 p.m. in London).

In markets where a public offering to individual investors is mandatory, the offering is then open for a period of 1 to 3 weeks for the public to subscribe following the close of institutional bookbuilding. Trading will start perhaps 4 days later. This method can leave underwriters at risk for a considerable period.

In essence, UK and European underwriters in traditional offerings own the securities they have underwritten and are at risk for many days. In the American system, and increasingly internationally, managers (although, confusingly, they are often called underwriters) are purchasers and distributors of shares, taking a risk for only a matter of hours.

## Fees and commissions

In international offerings commissions of 3.0 to 6.0% are common for corporate new issues. Privatisations generally have lower commissions. Usually, the larger the offering, the smaller the percentage commission. In international offerings, it is not uncommon for managers to pay their own expenses, including legal fees out of their commissions. In larger offerings, and in privatisations, the issuer may make a contribution to managers' expenses.

As competition among investment banks has intensified, so has downward pressure on the level of commissions. In 1997, large privatisations typically carried a total commission of slightly less than 3%. By 1999, some banks were willing to quote fees of less than 1%

of the transaction value for a large, prestigious privatisation. However, in the US, the standard fee for a small- to medium-sized ($50m to $150m) IPO has remained rock steady at 7.0%. By contrast, traditional UK fees for underwriting an offering are 2.0%.

Within the gross commission, or 'gross spread' to use the American term, fees are notionally divided three ways. Typically, 20% of the commission is called the *management fee*, which is meant to compensate the bookrunner for the work involved in organising the offering. Another 20% of the gross commission is called, somewhat misleadingly, the *underwriting fee*. All expenses incurred by managers in the completion of the offering are deducted from the 'underwriting' fee before it is paid. Usually, very little of the underwriting fee remains to be distributed to managers.

Finally, 60% of the gross commission is allocated to the selling concession, payable to the bank which sells the shares. The bookrunner has significant discretion on the allocation of shares and, hence, the selling concession among syndicate members. Typically, the bookrunner(s) will receive more than 50% of the total selling concession, ensuring that competition to win the bookrunner role is intense.

Underwriting and management fees are payable on the notional amount of stock that the syndicate member agrees to underwrite, while the selling fee relates to the amount of stock the syndicate member actually places.

# AFTER THE NEW ISSUE

## Stabilisation

Another feature of international offerings adapted from the US is the ability of the underwriter to stabilise the price of the shares immediately after pricing and allocation. Stabilisation is undertaken to facilitate the distribution of shares during the offering period and, typically, takes place for up to 30 days following allocation of the shares.

The lead manager may 'over-allot' shares (i.e., sell more shares than are being offered) to investors, thereby creating a short position in the market (i.e., the lead manager has sold shares which it doesn't own). If there is weakness in the price of the shares during the offering period, the lead manager can purchase shares in the market to 'fill' the short position, thereby creating demand for the shares and providing support for the market price.

To provide the lead manager and the underwriting syndicate with the maximum flexibility to support the offering in the aftermarket, it is typical for the company to grant a 'greenshoe' option. This option enables the underwriting syndicate to purchase additional shares (up to 15% of the total offering) from the company at the same price and on the same terms as the other shares offered for a period of 30 days. Therefore, if the share price rises in the month following the new issue, the lead manager would purchase shares from the greenshoe to cover its short position. If the share price falls, the greenshoe option is not exercised.

# Chapter

# 5

......................................

# RIGHTS ISSUES/
# SECONDARY
# OFFERINGS

Corporate financiers also have a key role to play when companies need to raise equity capital in the years following flotation. Companies raise money in order to invest in new capital expenditures or projects, to make acquisitions of other companies, to repay debt or simply when the market is good and they can opportunistically raise funds. Such subsequent equity financing can also be called *secondary offerings*, making it sometimes confusing with the term 'secondary offering' referring to the sale of shares by existing owners. In America, subsequent equity issues are referred to as 'seasoned' equity offerings.

In the UK, almost all subsequent equity offerings are done by way of a rights offering. The financier will advise the company on the amount to raise, the pricing and market conditions. As in flotations, the corporate finance team is responsible for the documentation, discussions with the regulators and overall co-ordination of the transaction team (solicitors, PR, stockbrokers, accountants).

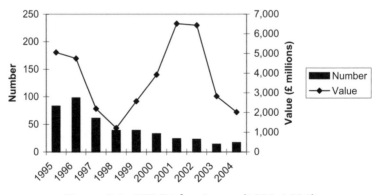

*Figure 5.1*   UK Rights Issues (1995–2004).

In a 'rights offering' (the term is used interchangeably with rights issue), all shareholders receive notification of the fundraising. If they wish to purchase the new shares, they do so (i.e., they exercise or take up their rights). If the shareholder does not wish to purchase the shares to which he is entitled, he can sell his rights on the Stock Exchange.

# PRE-EMPTION RIGHTS

Investors in UK Stock Exchange-quoted companies are protected from the dilution of their ownership stake through pre-emption rights. This means that if a firm wishes to raise new equity capital, it must first offer the shares it is planning to sell to its existing shareholders. The protection from dilution is as a result of both laws and strong traditions in the City. Assuming a shareholder 'takes up' her rights to subscribe to the new issue, she will maintain her proportionate share of the equity in the company.

An exemption to pre-emption practices exists in the UK. Companies are permitted to make an issue of up to 5% of shareholder's capital without offering the new shares first to existing shareholders.

Continental European companies can seek, and regularly receive, permission from their shareholders to waive pre-emption rights. Such pre-emption rights are not part of the corporate finance landscape in Canada or the US.

During the mid- to late-1990s, corporate financiers were at the centre of a debate over whether UK companies should change their approach to fundraising. Many people believed that pre-emption rules prevent new investors from achieving meaningful stakes in companies, thus narrowing the shareholder base and increasing dependence on a few investors. Many others argued that the *status quo* should be maintained.

A survey of UK finance directors into the system of rights issues and raising equity capital was conducted by MORI in 1998. Its main conclusion was that nearly 80% of finance directors believed that they should have access to a greater variety of financing methods.

When it came to the system of pre-emption rights, most supported the system, but thought that the 5% exemption was too low. One-third believed 10% was more appropriate, while 23% supported an exemption of up to 25%. Large-company finance directors generally found the current system most restrictive and half the finance directors (61% of FTSE 100 finance directors) believed that companies in other countries had a competitive advantage because of the flexibility of their systems.

The other side of the issue is represented by the following excerpt from a *Financial Times* article by Carol Galley, then co-head of Merrill Lynch Mercury Asset Management:

*... Pre-emptive rights are enshrined in law. They give existing shareholders first refusal on any new shares in a rights issue. Two things are central to this*

Table 5.1 Large UK rights issues.

| Company | Year | Amount raised (£m) |
|---|---|---|
| British Telecommunications | 2001 | 5,927 |
| Pearson | 2000 | 1,705 |
| BP | 1987 | 1,500 |
| Zeneca | 1993 | 1,300 |
| Eurotunnel | 1994 | 858 |
| ICI | 2002 | 800 |
| Allied-Lyons | 1994 | 670 |
| RMC Group | 1995 | 493 |
| Spirent | 2000 | 528 |
| Logica | 2000 | 463 |
| EMAP | 1998 | 368 |
| Scottish & Newcastle | 1995 | 364 |
| Misys | 1997 | 334 |

*principal: transfer of value and transfer of control. If shares are issued to new rather than existing shareholders there may be a transfer of value to the new shareholders from the existing ones. Whether this has actually happened can only be known with hindsight. In a pre-emptive issue no such transfer of value can take place. We therefore believe that pre-emptive issues are the correct way for companies to raise new equity and that proposals to permit more non-pre-emptive issues are misplaced.*

# SETTING THE PRICE

One of the most important aspects of a rights offering is setting the terms and the price of the new shares.

Typically, the new shares are offered at a discount to the prevailing trading price on the Stock Exchange. In most instances, the discount is set between 10 and 15%. For assurance, the issuing company will have the offer 'underwritten' – as in a flotation. This means that if the share price falls below the purchase price and the shareholders do not subscribe to the issue, the company is guaranteed to receive the funds.

The reason that offerings are underwritten is that they must remain open for 21 days. It is possible that the shares will fall below the issue price during this period. If so, no rational investor would purchase new shares when she could buy them in the market at a lower price.

## Calculating the theoretical rights price

For example, Bridge plc has 125 million shares outstanding, currently trading at 240p per share. The company needs £50 million to complete several projects and its corporate finance advisors have recommended a rights issue.

The advisors suggest an offering of 25 million shares at 200p per share (a discount of approximately 17% to the current price). The ratio of new shares to old is 25 : 125, meaning that for every five existing shares an investor owns, he is entitled to purchase one new share at 200p. This is referred to as a one for five rights issue (the ratio of 25 : 125 simplified). Rights issues can be done on the basis of any ratio (e.g., 1 for 4, 2 for 7, 3 for 11, etc.).

On issue, the share price is likely to fall from its current 240p, reflecting the new money raised and the new shares issued. The price at which the shares are likely to settle is referred to as the theoretical ex-rights price and is calculated as follows:

| | |
|---|---|
| Five existing shares at current price of 240p | 1,200 |
| One new share for cash at 200p | 200 |
| Value of six shares | 1,400 |
| Theoretical value of one share ex-rights (1,400/6) | 233p |

If a shareholder decides not to exercise his rights, he is able to sell the rights he has been sent on the Stock Exchange. The value of a right on one existing (old) share is:

$$\frac{TMV - SP}{n} = \frac{233 - 200}{5}$$

$$= 6.60p$$

where   $TMV$ = Theoretical market value of share ex-rights;

$SP$ = Subscription price;

$n$ = Number of old shares required to purchase one new share.

Therefore, the value of a right on one new share is equal to:

$$TMV - SP = 233 - 200$$

$$= 33p$$

This is the approximate price at which the rights should trade on the Stock Exchange during the issue period, other things being equal.

# RIGHTS ISSUE TIMETABLE

Rights issues follow a fairly standard timetable, leaving investors 21 days to decide whether to exercise their rights or to sell them in the stock market – rights become listed on the London Stock Exchange (*LSE*) or Alternative Investment Market (*AIM*) for their lifetime. Box 5.1 is a detailed timetable for the £5.9 billion rights offer launched by British Telecommunications plc (*BT*) in the spring of 2001.

## Fees and commissions

Traditionally, UK rights offerings carried a 2% commission. The total commission paid by the company raising the funds was divided as follows:

| | |
|---|---|
| Primary underwriter | 0.50% |
| Broker to the issue | 0.25% |
| Sub-underwriters | 1.25% |

The traditional fee structure mirrors that of the fee structure for UK flotations.

In 1996 the Office of Fair Trading began an investigation into the traditional split of fees – and particularly, the amount paid to sub-underwriters. This was as a response to a study conducted by academics at the London Business School which found that sub-underwriters were 'overpaid' for the risks taken in underwriting during the period 1986–1994.

| Box 5.1 Rights issue timetable. | |
| --- | --- |
| Record date for the Rights Issue | Close of business on 9 May |
| Nil Paid Rights and Fully Paid Rights enabled in CREST | By 8 a.m. on 21 May |
| Dealings in new BT Shares, nil paid, commence on the LSE | 8 a.m. on 21 May |
| Recommended latest time for requesting withdrawal of Nil Paid Rights from CREST | 4.30 p.m. on 7 June |
| Latest time for depositing renounced Provisional Allotment Letters, nil paid, into CREST or for dematerialising Nil Paid Rights into a CREST stock account | 3 p.m. on 11 June |
| Latest time and date for splitting Provisional Allotment Letters | 3 p.m. on 12 June |
| Dealings in new BT Shares, fully paid, commence on the LSE | 8 a.m. on 14 June |
| Latest time and date for acceptance | 9.30 a.m. on 15 June |
| Recommended latest time and date for requesting withdrawal of Fully Paid Rights from CREST | 4.30 p.m. on 22 June |
| Latest time and date for splitting Provisional Allotment Letters, fully paid | 3 p.m. on 27 June |
| Latest time for depositing renounced Provisional Allotment Letters, fully paid into CREST or for dematerialising Fully Paid Rights into a CREST stock account | 3 p.m. on 27 June |
| Latest time and date for registration of renunciation of Provisional Allotment Letters, fully paid | 3 p.m. on 29 June |
| New BT Shares credited to CREST stock accounts | 2 July |
| Despatch of definitive share certificates for new BT Shares | By 16 July |

In response, since 1996, sub-underwriters have been invited (by the primary underwriter or sponsor) to 'bid' or tender for the fee they require to take up any shares that remain as a result of unexercised rights. This has resulted in a general decrease in the sub-underwriting portion of the total commission.

The first issue which included a tender for sub-underwriting occurred in 1996 as part of a £222 million rights issue for Stakis, the hotels group. Corporate financiers at Schroders devised a method whereby institutions who were interested in sub-underwriting the issue tendered for the fee that they would receive for doing so. One-third of the sub-underwriting fees were put out to tender, which resulted in bids that saved the company approximately £400,000 in underwriting commissions.

In October 1997, Schroders put the sub-underwriting for all of a £125 million rights issue for Berkeley out to tender. In that offer, the shares were offered at a discount of 26% to the previous market price in order to reduce risk to the sub-underwriters – in most cases, the discount is set at 10–15%. This resulted in the sub-underwriting commission being cut from its 'standard' 1.25% to 0.3%, saving Berkeley nearly £1.2 million.

Finally, in April 1998, Monument Oil and Gas did away with underwriters altogether by getting its leading shareholders to underwrite the issue, rather than engaging an underwriter and sub-underwriter. In doing so, the company saved itself £1.3 million in commissions on its

£96 million rights issue. Monument was able to do so because it had relatively few, large shareholders who were long-term supporters of the company. Institutional investors representing 54% of share capital took up their rights, leaving only 46% of the issue to be underwritten. The commission on the remainder of the issue was 0.625%, less than half the 1.75% combined underwriting and sub-underwriting fees. The one for four rights issue was priced at a 10% discount to the share price prior to announcement.

### Deep discounted rights issues

One way to avoid paying underwriting commissions is the use of a deep discounted rights issue. This type of issue sets the price of the new shares at much greater than the 10–15% discount noted above. Companies have tended to shy away from deep discounted rights issues for several reasons. In particular, many believed they would be under pressure to maintain the level of dividends on the enlarged equity, increasing their cost of capital.

Deep discounted issues are relatively uncommon in the UK, although as the following paragraphs describe, the second largest rights issue ever completed was done at a 50% discount.

On Monday, 31 July 2000 Pearson announced a takeover bid of $2.5 billion (£1.66 billion) for a US company called National Computer Systems (NCS) which is involved in education services. To finance the acquisition, one of many made by Pearson in 2000, the company announced a £1.7 billion rights issue on the basis of three new shares for every 11 owned at a price of £10 per new share – 170 million new shares were issued. The price of £10 was a discount of approximately 50% to the prevailing share price of £20.10.

One of the reasons Pearson decided to offer a deep discounted rights issue was that it was able to minimise the commissions paid. In deep discounted issues, it is unusual for an investor not to participate, and some dispense with underwriting completely. In Pearson's case, it decided to underwrite £1.5 billion of the total (organised by Goldman Sachs and Cazenove) which ensured that the bulk of the funds would be available on closing. The cost of the underwriting was 0.5% of the funds raised or £7.5 million in total. If the issue had been underwritten on standard terms, Pearson would have paid £35 million in commissions. At the time, institutions backed the move which they described as 'innovative' and 'cost-effective'.

# SECONDARY OFFERINGS

In countries where pre-emption rights do not exist or are regularly waived by investors, companies requiring equity capital have two choices: a marketed offering or a 'bought deal'.

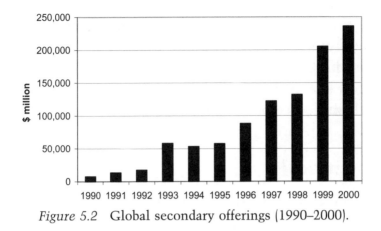

*Figure 5.2*   Global secondary offerings (1990–2000).

# Marketed offerings

Marketed secondary offerings are structured in a manner very similar to an Initial Public Offering (*IPO*). The marketed offering is the most common method of raising funds in the US. The company appoints an investment bank and assembles a team of lawyers, accountants and PR experts. Corporate financiers co-ordinate the preparation of a prospectus and take soundings in the market regarding investor appetite for the new shares. Confidentiality is important in marketed offerings as information regarding a firm's impending sale of shares would cause a fall in the company's share price.

Once the preliminary prospectus is prepared and filed with the regulator a marketing campaign commences. Marketing for a secondary offering is less extensive than that for a company's IPO as investors are already familiar with the firm's business. Where an IPO often has a 4–6-week marketing period, a secondary offering typically uses 1–3 weeks.

Once the regulator approves the offering documents, and the lead manager has sufficient orders, the lead manager closes the book and prices the new issue. The price of the new shares is usually set at a very small discount to the closing price on the pricing day.

## Bought deals

A bought deal, sometimes referred to as a 'block trade', involves a bank buying shares in a company, using its own capital, and then selling the shares as quickly as possible to institutional investors. The difference between the buying and selling price is the investment bank's profit.

A bought deal is more risky for an investment bank (compared with an offering using bookbuilding) because it can suffer losses if it is unable to sell the shares. Vendors like bought deals, because they are faster than formal offerings (rarely taking more than 24 hours for successful transactions). On the other hand, the vendor must accept that it will likely have to sell its shares at a discount to the prevailing market price. The discount is required because of the need for speed and secrecy as well as the fact that the investment bank is risking its own capital.

Bought deals typically work best when a small proportion of the total capital of the company's shares are being sold (i.e., less than 5%), the company is well known with a research following and there is a liquid market in the shares.

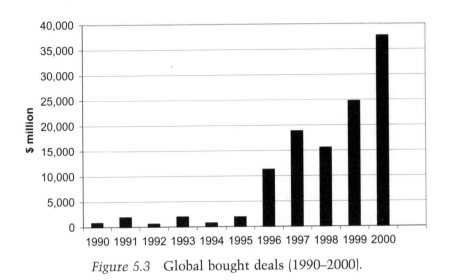

*Figure 5.3*   Global bought deals (1990–2000).

## Bought deal example

In 1995, the UK Government hired NM Rothschild, the merchant bank, to advise it on the sale of the state's remaining holdings in a number of privatised companies. These were worth approximately £1.2 billion. The largest holding was a 1.8% stake in British Petroleum (BP), valued at over £500 million in December 1995.

Late in the year, Rothschild was ready to move. On Friday afternoon, 1 December, the firm received approval for its plan from the Treasury. Following a weekend of fine-tuning their strategy, corporate finance and equity capital markets professionals were sure of its success.

On Monday, a number of leading investment banks in London were invited to Rothschild's offices at 8 p.m. after the markets in London and New York had closed.

The firms were not told which of the stocks they were bidding for until after they had arrived. The only indication they had been given in advance was that they would be called upon to commit a large amount of capital.

Rothschild kept the bidders apart all evening. After being told that they were bidding for the government's entire stake in BP, each investment bank was given 2 hours to respond. The winner was SBC Warburg (now UBS Investment Bank) which bid 508p per share for 101 million shares – just over £513 million. This compared with the closing price of 531p, a 4.15% discount. Other bidders were said to be BZW (Barclays), Merrill Lynch and at least one other American house, each of whom had offered less than 508p per share.

When trading opened on Tuesday, 5 December, Warburg's salesmen called institutions throughout the UK and Europe and at lunch-time began to offer shares to US investors, as they arrived in their offices. The holding was placed with approximately 100 institutions, split evenly between the UK and Europe, and the US, at a price of 513p. BP shares closed at 517p, down 14p on the day, but still above the re-offer price.

For the day's work and the use of the firm's capital, Warburg earned approximately £5 million.

## Accelerated bookbuilding

Accelerated bookbuilding is a variant on the bought deal. A company that is reasonably well known, with good liquidity in its shares, may opt for a shortened marketing period, rather than the typical 2–3 weeks as in a traditional marketed offering. In an accelerated book-building, the investment bank(s) may organise only two or three roadshow presentations in order to build demand for the shares over 2 or 3 days. In some cases, if the company is well enough known, the bankers can do away with the requirement for investor presentations altogether.

In February 2000, National Grid, in an extremely well-timed move, reduced its holding in the telecommunications and Internet company, Energis from 46% to 36% via an offer using accelerated bookbuilding. The sale of 30 million shares raised £1,014 million (before costs, commissions and taxes) for the parent company.

During January and February shares in all European tele-communications companies had been rising. The week before the sale of Energis shares was announced, its share price had increased by an extraordinary 30% to £37.97 each. At the opening of the UK market on Wednesday, 9 February, National Grid announced that it had hired ABN Amro Rothschild leading a small syndicate of banks which included Cazenove, Dresdner Kleinwort Benson and HSBC to sell up to 30 million shares.

On announcement of the accelerated bookbuilding, the shares dropped to £33.63, below the price that the banks were offering the shares (£33.80). However, by the end of the day all 30 million shares had been placed at the offer price.

# DEMERGERS

A demerger occurs when a parent company distributes shares in a subsidiary to its (the parent's) shareholders. On completion of a demerger, the two publicly traded companies will have identical shareholder lists. A demerger can be completed in conjunction with a capital raising for the subsidiary as in the case of the ICI–ZENECA demerger in 1993 in the UK. To illustrate, if an investor had owned 2% of ICI shares prior to the demerger, she would own 2% of ICI and 2% of ZENECA following the demerger.

Corporate finance teams are called upon to help companies determine the most appropriate structure for demerged entities. Their knowledge of how institutional investors are likely to react is extremely important to chief executives and finance directors. Once the structure is in place, corporate financiers co-ordinate the documentation and other aspects of the demerged firm's introduction to the Stock Exchange.

In 1997, British Gas demerged its pipeline network and international operations from its domestic gas distribution business. Then in 2000, management announced the demerger of the international operations (Lattice) from its pipeline network (BG).

In September 2000 Kingfisher, a UK retail group, announced that it was to split in two in early 2001. Its domestic general merchandise case chains (Woolworths and Superdrug) would form one company, while its pan-European DIY and electricals businesses (Comet, B&Q, Darty and Castorama) would form the second.

# Chapter

# 6

. . . . . . . . . . . . . . . . . . . . . . . . . . . . . . . . .

# MERGERS AND ACQUISITIONS

O ne of the main roles of the corporate financier is to initiate, execute and complete corporate acquisitions. Corporate financiers act as advisors to the most senior management and the Boards of Directors in major Mergers and Acquisitions (M&A) transactions. Despite the increase in the number of transactions in the past two decades, mergers are still not an everyday occurrence at most companies. Thus, corporate management requires the assistance and knowledge of professionals who have advised on many deals in the past.

The terms 'merger', 'acquisition' and 'takeover' tend to be used interchangeably, although there are specific definitions for accounting purposes.

Mergers affect all industries and all countries. Many deals involved bidders from one country acquiring a target in another (e.g., Pernod Ricard's (FR) $17.8 billion acquisition of Allied Domecq (UK) or Suez (FR) paying $13.9 billion for Belgium's Electrabel). Other deals are notable for their sheer size (e.g., the Time Warner–AOL stock swap valued at more than $200 billion at the time it was announced in 2000).

Figure 6.1 illustrates that, even in a 'slow' year, more than $1.3 trillion in deals are completed.

# RATIONALE FOR M&A

Management give a number of reasons for entering into an M&A. One of the main reasons is to enable the

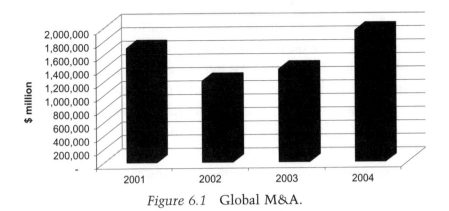

*Figure 6.1* Global M&A.

company to grow more quickly than it could through organic growth. The growth may come from geographic expansion or the ability to offer new products and services or to reach new customers.

For technology-driven companies, the ability to capture a specific component or broaden its technical base can lead to transactions. For example, Cisco Systems, best known for manufacturing the routers and other equipment on which Internet traffic depends, made 70 acquisitions between 1993 and 2000.

Until the 1990s, many companies, known as conglomerates (e.g., Hanson, BET, Tomkins) were built on acquisitions. Senior management at these conglomerates felt that they had superior management skills and disciplines which could add value to their companies.

Using excess cash is also sometimes viewed as the reason behind acquisitions, although management of the acquiring company would not admit to this.

The only appropriate rationale for M&A is if the transaction(s) create value for the shareholders of the company. This may be through strengthening of the business, either by acquiring new or better products or better management. Value-creating acquisitions are almost always in industries of which the acquiring company already has a good understanding. Diversification for its own sake rarely creates sustainable value.

The senior corporate financier will often be involved in corporate discussions regarding the decision to undertake a transaction. Corporate financiers typically have a better sense of investor opinion of (specific) transactions as well as an understanding of the types of deals being done in other industrial sectors.

At this early stage, a junior corporate financier may be asked to assemble data on a wide range of potential targets or partners. While the bankers do valuations of these other businesses, the corporate executives are examining them from the perspective of strategic fit.

## TYPES OF MERGER

Mergers (and acquisitions) are typically classified as one of the following:

- *Horizontal mergers* join companies that operate in similar lines of business. BP and Amoco in oil and gas; Total, Fina and Elf Aquitaine in the same industry; Royal Bank of Scotland and National Westminster Bank in banking; Sanofi and Aventis and, finally, Glaxo and Wellcome – subsequently, GlaxoWellcome with SmithKline Beecham to form GlaxoSmithKline – in pharmaceuticals. Horizontal mergers or takeovers allow the enlarged company to benefit from economies of scale and the ability to cut costs.

- *Vertical mergers* bring companies either closer to their customers or closer to their source of supply. The purchase of automobile dealers by manufacturers such as Ford and Vauxhall and others is an example. Ford also acquired Hertz, the care hire agency, but divested this subsidiary in 2005 for $15 billion to a buy-out group.

- *Diversification or conglomerate* mergers join companies operating in unrelated businesses. Managers of conglomerates make the claim that their business model allows for the more effective use of central services such as accounting and taxation and the ability to smooth earnings over a business cycle. During the 1990s and 2000s investors turned against conglomerates and conglomerate mergers, causing many of the conglomerates built up during the 1960s, 1970s and 1980s to be split apart. While the building of conglomerates created wealth for shareholders – for a time – the real winners were corporate financiers who aided first in the building (acquisitions) and later in the destruction (disposals) of the conglomerates. Of course, fees were payable in all transactions.

- *Financial acquisitions* are driven by the financial logic of the transaction. In general, financial mergers fall under the category of *Management Buyouts* (*MBOs*) or *Leveraged Buyouts* (*LBOs*) and related names. The backers of such transactions are not generally long-term investors and there may be no strategic logic behind them. MBOs and LBOs are discussed more fully in Chapter 7.

- *Ego-driven* or 'me too' mergers are often initiated by chief executives in an industry who see others entering into mergers and decide that an M&A is necessary to the success of his company without thinking through the strategic logic.

# MERGER WAVES

During the past century, five separate merger 'waves' have been identified by observers. The first three were very much US phenomena, while the last two waves have been more global in nature. The most recent merger wave, still in progress as this book is being written, has a very large European component.

During the 1890s, the first merger wave saw some of the nascent industries (rail, oil, steel) consolidate. This wave continued in the US until the end of that century. A further wave of industry consolidation took place during the 1920s in both the UK and the US. Industries such as automotive manufacturing coalesced around key manufacturers.

Between 1967 and 1969 a large number of 'conglomerate' mergers took place in the US. Most of the offerings were made on a share for share basis, with the fastest growing conglomerates able to offer the most attractive terms, as their shares were most highly rated (i.e., they exchanged high PE ratio shares for low).

In the late 1980s the first round of financial mergers took place. These were a result of cheap and plentiful credit and many corporations willing to sell non-core businesses (many of which had been acquired in the conglomerate merger boom). The pinnacle, and for many, the end of the boom, was the acquisition of RJR Nabisco by the New York LBO firm Kohlberg, Kravis & Roberts (*KKR*). *Barbarians at the Gate* is an excellent description of the transaction.

The 1990s merger wave continued into the next century. From 1994 to 2000, companies in industries as varied as banking, pharmaceuticals, telecommunications and oil and gas have been merging to gain size and 'critical mass'. After a brief respite following the bursting of the Internet bubble, M&A activity has increased again (see Figure 6.1). One of the main differences about the final wave of the 20th century is that it involved companies making significant cross-border acquisitions.

# FINANCING THE TRANSACTION

There are three main alternatives to financing an acquisition. The bidder can offer cash for the shares of the target, it can offer its own shares or it can offer a combination of the two. Other alternatives, such as offering debt securities and preference shares, are also possible, but used less frequently as they tend to complicate the

decision the target shareholders must make regarding
the value of the offer.

During the 1980s' merger wave, numerous transactions
involved a complicated mix of securities offered in consideration for the target's shares. This often made evaluating competing offers extremely difficult. Unique among
these securities were Payment In Kind (*PIK*) bonds.
Bidders would offer target shareholders partial payment
in PIK bonds – bonds that paid, in lieu of interest, only
more of the same bonds.

Many mergers during the telecoms/Internet mania involved swapping one company's overvalued shares for
another's – no cash involved. Since the bursting of the
bubble, cash has become the preferred consideration in
takeovers.

All cash offers have a number of advantages. The price to
be received by the selling shareholder is obvious and
easily quantified. The selling shareholders can use the
cash received to reinvest as they please – they are not
forced to become shareholders of the bidder. By offering
cash, the bidding company does not dilute the ownership position of its current shareholders as would happen
if it offered shares to the target. One disadvantage to a
cash offer is that it triggers a sale and potential capital
gains tax liability for the selling shareholders.

The advantages to offering shares in an acquisition are
largely the opposite of the cash offer. Target company
shareholders are able to defer any capital gains tax liability until they sell the shares of the merged entity, at

their own timing. In addition, the target shareholders are able to maintain an interest in the ongoing business of the new company.

## Bootstrap transactions

Many investors and stock market commentators focus on the impact an acquisition or merger has on the successor firm's Earnings Per Share (*EPS*). In some cases, the source of financing for the transaction will have an immediate impact on EPS. For example, if the acquisition takes place in early 2006, the accountants prepare a *pro forma* income statement, which shows the EPS of the acquiror had it owned the target for all of 2005. This would include the additional revenues, costs and, most importantly, the additional interest expense incurred by taking on debt to make the transaction. As the thinking goes, if the acquisition is 'accretive' to earnings and EPS (i.e., increases), the transaction is a good one. If it is dilutive to earnings, the deal is bad.

Where equity is to be used (i.e., in a merger, or an acquisition where shares are offered), the effect on EPS is immediate and will be examined by analysts and investors. As a general rule if the existing Price Earnings (*PE*) ratio of the acquirer is higher than the 'exit PE' at which the target is acquired, the acquirer will show, on a *pro forma* basis, an immediate enhancement of EPS. This effect is often referred to as the bootstrap effect. If the acquirer's PE is lower than the target's PE, dilution results.

*Between 1966 and 1972 faddish conglomerates used high-priced stocks to acquire a wild assortment of companies. Often they were able to create the illusion of growth by using their high-multiple stocks to buy low-multiple companies. If such a deal is accounted for as 'pooling' rather than a 'purchase', the effect is to give an artificial boost to the earnings per share of the acquirer. But once the dealing pace slows – and investors finally see through the accounting – the magical growth vanishes.*

Forbes Global, 16 October 2000

# REGULATION OF M&As

In the M&A business, one of the most important functions of the corporate financier is to ensure that the deal timing, structure, etc, adheres to local rules and regulations.

Mergers, acquisitions and takeovers involving public companies in the UK are subject to regulation by the *Panel on Takeovers and Mergers* (the Takeover Panel) and the Financial Services Authority (prior to 2000, the London Stock Exchange was responsible).

The Takeover Panel (a self-regulatory organisation) is responsible for the *City Code on Takeovers and Mergers*, published in a blue binder and, hence, popularly known as the *Blue Book*. The *Blue Book* is a voluntary Code which does not have the force of law, but reflects the opinions of professionals involved in M&As. The Code provides a framework under which acquisitions and mergers of publicly quoted companies can take place and is designed to ensure fair treatment of all shareholders in an acquisition.

In the UK, when monopoly and anti-trust considerations arise because of the size of the participants in a transaction, the *Office of Fair Trading (OFT)* can refer the transaction to the *Competition Commission (CC)* for review. If the CC finds that a monopoly may be created to the detriment of the public interest, it refers the decision to the Secretary of State for Trade for final resolution. Very large mergers or those with cross-border implications are subject to vetting by the EU. Such referrals can take considerable time and any bid's timetable is deemed to have been suspended until competition issues have been resolved.

## Key elements of the City Code

The authors of the Code realised that it was impossible to devise rules in sufficient detail to cover all eventualities that might arise in a transaction. Thus, it is a collection of specific rules and general principles. The Code's general thrust is set out in the paragraph below:

*Each director of an offeror and of the offeree company has a responsibility to ensure that the Code is complied with in the conduct of an offer. Financial advisors have a particular responsibility to comply with the Code and to ensure that an offeror and the offeree company, and their respective directors, are aware of their responsibilities under the Code and will comply with them. Financial advisors should ensure that the Panel is consulted whenever relevant and should co-operate fully with any enquiries made by the Panel. Financial advisors must also be mindful of conflicts of interest.*

Selected general principles:

- All shareholders of the same class of an offeree company must be treated similarly by an offeror.
- During the course of an offer neither an offeror nor the offeree company, nor any of their respective advisors, may furnish information to some shareholders which is not made available to all shareholders. This principle does not apply to the furnishing of information in confidence by the offeree company to a *bona fide* potential offeror or *vice versa*.
- Shareholders must be given sufficient information and advice to enable them to reach a properly informed decision and must have sufficient time to do so. No relevant information should be withheld from them.
- All parties to an offer must use every endeavour to prevent the creation of a false market in the securities of an offeror or the offeree company. Parties involved in offers must take care that statements are not made which may mislead shareholders or the market.
- Rights of control must be exercised in good faith and the oppression of a minority is wholly unacceptable.
- Where control of a company is acquired by a person, or persons acting in concert, a general offer to all

other shareholders is normally required; a similar obligation may arise if control is consolidated.

At the time of writing, UK officials were attempting to determine how to integrate the EU Takeover Directive consistently with the Code.

# Chapter

# 7

......................................

# MANAGEMENT BUYOUTS

A *Management Buyout* (*MBO*) is a specific type of Mergers and Acquisition (*M&A*) transaction. An MBO occurs when a team of managers purchase a company, subsidiary, division or business unit from its existing owner. They typically borrow a large portion of the purchase price. A *Management Buyin* (*MBI*) occurs when an external team of managers purchase a company, subsidiary, division or business unit from its existing owner. An *Institutional Buyout* (*IBO*) is a buyout instigated and led by a private equity fund (institution). Management is either retained following the acquisition or new managers are brought in on closing.

All buyouts typically borrow a large portion of the purchase price. Thus, they are referred to as *Leveraged Buyouts* (*LBOs*) in the US. The underlying principle behind all the variants of buyout is the use of the business's cash flows to pay for the debt incurred to finance the purchase. Over time, the business pays for itself.

The US provides the largest buyout market globally, although the European market for deals is rapidly catching up. Within Europe, the UK is the largest market for buyouts by a large order of magnitude (see Figure 7.1), but continental transactions are increasing.

As noted above, the purchaser is using the future cash flows of the business to pay down the debt assumed on the buyout which was used to fund the purchase price. The following example (Box 7.1) describes the core financial elements of an hypothetical MBO.

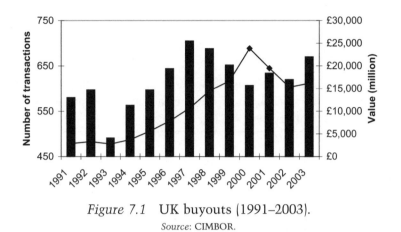

*Figure 7.1*    UK buyouts (1991–2003).
*Source:* CIMBOR.

---

*Box 7.1*    Example.

Assume that a company has gross assets of £80 million, total liabilities of £60 million and, therefore, net assets (shareholders' equity) of £20 million. Assume that an MBO takes place for a purchase price equal to the net assets of the firm, or £20 million. The purchase will be funded by borrowing against the assets of the company.

Immediately following completion of the buyout, the balance sheet would show £80 million of gross assets as before and £80 million of liabilities, including the £20 million of borrowings assumed to make the purchase. Thus, net assets are £0. The MBO team now owns a business with equity that is worth zero (at least on the balance sheet).

During the ensuing years, the company's business will continue to generate profits and cash flows. Suppose that by the end of year 3, £20 million of net profits and cash had been generated. The balance sheet now has £80 million in gross assets, £60 million of liabilities and, having repaid the £20 million borrowed to buy the company, £20 million in net assets.

At the end of year 3, the owners have equity with a book value of £20 million. They have used the cash-generative capability of the company to repay the debt of £20 million assumed on closing of the transaction, thereby creating value of £20 million for themselves over a 3-year period.

One of the main prerequisites for a successful buyout is the purchase of predictable cash flows at a reasonable price – something that is not always possible.

# FINANCIAL STRUCTURE

The organisers of a buyout first determine how much bank finance can be used in the transaction. They then add the (relatively small) amount of equity provided by the management team to the bank debt. At this stage the institutional equity providers calculate their expected return, based on the risk of the transaction and the amount of equity they are required to invest to meet the purchase price. If the combination of bank debt, management equity and private equity is not sufficient to purchase the business, the organisers will turn to mezzanine financiers to fill the gap.

Figure 7.2 is sometimes referred to as the funding triangle. It represents the total funding required for the MBO, including working capital requirements.

When funding a buyout, one starts at the bottom layer: bank debt. Generally, the entrepreneur trying to fund a buyout attempts to get as much bank debt as possible because it is cheaper than other forms of finance. The relative costs of finance are covered in Chapter 9.

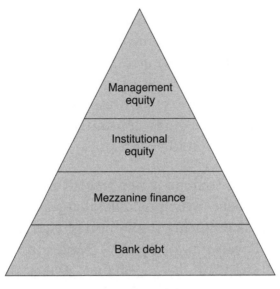

*Figure 7.2*  Typical funding structure.

Frequently, banks will lend only on a secured basis – i.e., they must have direct claim over the assets of the business. Because they are lending on a secured basis, the interest rate charged by a bank (or syndicate of banks) is relatively low. During the decade from 1995 to 2005, the average amount of bank debt in transactions ranged from a low of around 40% at the tail end of the early 1990s' recession to a high of slightly more than 50% of total value.

We next move from the base of the triangle to the top which represents the small amount that management will invest in the shares of the company. Their investment is pure risk capital and rarely comprises more than 10% of the funding pyramid. In-between the bank finance and management equity is the institutional equity 'tranche'.

The amount of equity invested by institutional investors –
private equity funds and venture capitalists – will vary by
transaction and the perceived risk. Most private equity
investors aim to earn a return of 25% to 40% on their
portfolio of investments. During the decade 1995 to
2005, institutional equity accounted for between 30%
and 40% of total transaction value.

The mezzanine tranche is not present in all buyouts. It
is unsecured debt, which usually charges a high interest
rate as well as requiring some form of equity, usually in
the form of warrants or options. Mezzanine finance is
normally supplied by specialist financing groups.
Mezzanine finance typically ranges from 0% to as
much as 20% of transactions in which it is sought.


# BANK FINANCE
# (SECURED LENDING)

The level of bank financing depends on four areas: the
security available, the interest cover, the gearing ratio
and the cash cover.

The first stage is the examination of the fixed and
current assets of the business where the bank will
assess their quality and security for lending purposes.
For instance, a firm whose customers are major multi-
nationals will have a higher quality debtors' book than a
firm concentrating on sales to local owner–operators.
Thus, banks will be prepared to lend against a higher
proportion of the former than the latter.

With respect to coverage ratios, the banks look at profit before interest tax and depreciation and divided by the expected amount of interest expense. As described by Brealey and Myers (2000), 'The regular interest payment is a hurdle that companies must keep jumping if they are to avoid default. The [interest coverage] ratio measures how much clear air there is between hurdler and hurdle.' A ratio of 2.5 times or so is generally the minimum acceptable level. The gearing ratio (debt to equity ratio) is also examined. Maximum gearing is 140%, as a result of Bank of England rules.

Finally, the banks will want to know that they can be repaid from the forecast cash flow of the business. In early 2000, the maximum period for loans to UK buyouts was approximately 8 years, while a couple of years previously the maximum period was 5 years. The variation is a result of changes in the perception of risk, future economic conditions and competition among banks to make loans.

The interest rate charged will vary with market conditions and the quality of security offered, but a range of London Inter-Bank Offer Rate (*LIBOR*) + 200 basis points to LIBOR + 400 basis points gives you the idea (remember from Chapter 2, LIBOR is the rate at which banks lend funds to each other). During economic boom times, when lenders are confident and competition to win business is high, the interest rate will be at the low end of this range and occasionally below. During less prosperous times, the interest rate charged will trend upwards.

In 1998, the size of the European leveraged lending market was $36 billion. It leapt to $96 billion the following year, before levelling off in 2000. By 2004, the value of the market had hit nearly $250 million. Bankers involved in the business say that the trend toward corporate focus and restructuring was the main driver of LBOs and leveraged loans.

At the time of writing, some of the most active participants in the European leveraged loan market were: JP Morgan, Citibank, Royal Bank of Scotland, Deutsche Bank, Barclays and Bank of America. In addition, 'traditional' investment banks such as Goldman Sachs and Lehman Brothers had joined the market in a major way.

# PRIVATE EQUITY FUNDS

Private equity firms tend to look to make an Internal Rate of Return (*IRR*) of between 25% and 40% over the holding period of between 3 and 7 years. Like bank lenders, competition among equity funders will drive the required returns to the lower end of the range, and occasionally below. In recessionary times, private equity houses will require higher returns.

In all cases, the equity providers will evaluate the risk of the business carefully before advancing funds. The above figures are for average risks and for illustration only.

At the end of 2005, private equity firms in Europe were estimated to have over €140 billion of funds available.

Table 7.1   Selected UK private equity providers.

| | |
|---|---|
| 3i Group | Cazenove |
| Advent | CVC Capital Partners |
| Alchemy Partners | Electra Partners |
| Apax Partners | ECI Partners |
| Barclays Private Equity | HSBC Private Equity |
| Candover | Permira |

Assuming an average equity portion of transactions of 40%, over €350 billion of transactions were theoretically possible. In fact, some private equity specialists complain that there is too much competition for deals and that they are unable to achieve the returns that they have been used to historically.

During 2004, European private equity providers reported an average return of 24.88% according to a Strategic Capital Management (SCM) survey. Institutions earn their return from three sources:

- the running yield on the sums invested, typically by way of a preference share dividend;
- repayment of capital over time;
- sale of the holding in the company on exit – to a trade buyer, to another private equity fund or when the company goes public.

# MEZZANINE FINANCE

Medium-sized companies have used mezzanine debt for many years in both Europe and the US as an alternative to high-yield bonds or bank debt. The product ranks between senior bank debt and equity in a company's capital structure, and mezzanine investors take higher risks than bond investors, but expect to earn a higher return – typically between 15% and 20%.

Companies that are too small to use the bond markets – either traditional or high yield – often turn to mezzanine funders. This feature, plus the ability to structure each deal more than a bond issue, makes mezzanine a popular source of LBO financing.

Mezzanine is riskier than bank debt as illustrated by the highly levered purchase of Finelist – a car parts distributor – by a French competitor, Autodis, in early 2000. The buyout, which had a total value of €505 million, was financed with leveraged loans and €275 million of mezzanine debt. In early autumn 2000, Finelist broke several financial covenants and entered receivership. While the holders of senior debt financing were able to recover the amounts lent, those who had participated in the mezzanine level were left with significant losses.

## HIGH-YIELD BONDS

High-yield bonds are bonds issued by companies with a credit rating below what is called *investment grade*. Investment grade ratings are anything above BBB/Baa (as rated by Moody's or Standard & Poor's). A high-yield bond, as one might expect, generally carries a high coupon offering the investor a high yield to maturity.

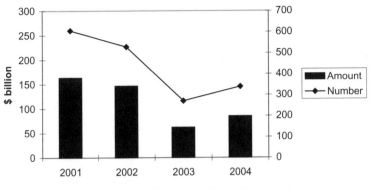

*Figure 7.3* Global high-yield debt new issues.

Many bank loans in LBOs are refinanced using the high-yield market, as the rates are competitive and borrowers can gain access to funds for longer periods than banks are willing to commit to making a loan. In most cases, banks refuse to extend long-term fixed rate loans to non-investment grade borrowers. When bank credit is available, it is typically offered only on a floating rate basis at punitive interest rates.

The European high-yield market grew rapidly during the latter half of the 1990s, fuelled by an explosion of issues by telecommunications companies. It continues to be dwarfed by the high-yield market in the US, which accounts for as much as 90% of global new issues of high-yield bonds. Figure 7.3 illustrates the number and volume of high-yield debt new issues in recent years.

# Part

# II

...........................................

# CORPORATE FINANCE TECHNIQUES

During the early stages of a corporate financier's career, one of the most frequent tasks he will be faced with is the valuation of a company, a division or its securities. Valuation underpins the price at which an Initial Public Offering (*IPO*) is launched. Valuation is vital in determining the price to offer for a business in an acquisition or merger. Valuation of the different securities offered in a Management Buyout/Leveraged Buyout (*MBO/LBO*) can mean the difference between a completed transaction and a busted deal.

Part II of the book introduces the main tools used in the daily life of a corporate financier: the tools needed to understand how to value businesses and their securities. These chapters are concerned with the techniques used to value businesses for the transactions listed in Part I, as well as for determining whether securities are accurately priced in the secondary market. Chapter 8 presents the most common methods used to value securities: cash flow based and comparables or relative valuations. Chapter 9 covers the determination of the discount rate used in cash flow based valuations, while Chapter 10 introduces the concept of Shareholder Value Added or economic profit.

The following chapters assume that the reader is familiar with corporate financial statements – i.e., the balance sheet, and profit and loss statement. We also assume a basic understanding of the principles of the concept of present value.

This chapter introduces two of the most popular equity valuation approaches: discounted cash flow, and comparable or relative valuations. The Appendix, which contains the results of a survey of UK corporate financiers, shows that these are the most frequently relied upon methods of valuation. Other specialised valuation methods are available to corporate financiers (e.g., asset valuations, option-based models), but we leave these to more specialised texts.

We begin by examining the process of bond valuation. Bonds and other fixed interest securities are relatively easy to value, because they promise a fixed stream of interest payments on known dates in the future. Equities, on the other hand, have a much greater degree of uncertainty regarding future dividends and capital appreciation. However, the principles of bond valuation underlie one of the most important business valuation methods.

## VALUING BONDS

The core business valuation techniques in use today are derived from the pricing of bonds with fixed interest coupons. An understanding of bond pricing will provide the reader with a grounding in the fundamentals of Discounted Cash Flow (*DCF*) valuation. To understand the price of a bond, or any promise to pay a sum of money in the future, one starts with the concept of present value.

The simplest way to start is to look at a security that makes only one payment in the future: a zero-coupon bond, introduced in Chapter 2, fits the bill. As you will recall, the zero-coupon bond derives its name from the fact that there are no interest payments made during the life of the bond. The only cash flows involved are the amount the purchaser pays up front – the price of the bond – and the amount paid by the issuer on maturity – the redemption amount.

For example, a company issues 10-year bonds at a price of £385 per £1,000 face value. This means that the company receives £385 today, but must repay its investors £1,000 in 10 years' time. It is clear that zero coupons are not a source of free capital.

The yield to maturity (and hence, the effective interest rate being paid by the issuer) is calculated using the following formula:

$$P = \frac{M}{(1+r)^n}$$

where     $P =$ Price;
              $M =$ Maturity value (redemption amount);
              $r =$ Yield to maturity;
              $n =$ Number of years to maturity.

Therefore, the yield to maturity on the bond with a price of £385, 10 years to maturity and maturity value of £1,000 is calculated as follows:

$$385 = \frac{1,000}{(1+r)^{10}}$$

By using a financial calculator or computer spreadsheet, $r$ is calculated as approximately 10% per annum. Thus, the investor earns 10% compounded annually on her purchase of the zero-coupon bond. At the same time, we can see that it *costs* the company 10% per year to have use of the investor's loan.

For coupon bonds, today's value or price is the present value of the future payments (interest coupon and the return of capital on maturity) discounted by the yield to maturity:

$$P = \sum \frac{CF_n}{(1+r)^n}$$

*CF* represents both coupon and principal repayment on maturity

*Risk*: the discount rate $r$ is adjusted for risk

where   $\sum$ = Sum of cash flows;
   $CF_n$ = Cash flow received in period $n$ (coupon payment and principal repayment);
   $r$ = Yield to maturity (discount rate);
   $P$ = Principal amount to be repaid on maturity (sometimes called *par value*).

Box 8.1 illustrates the pricing of a new bond issue.

# VALUING SHARES AND COMPANIES

There are numerous definitions of value when approaching equity valuation. The economic, or intrinsic, value of a business represents its value to the current owner or to a prospective owner (e.g., in an M&A deal). It is not necessarily the price at which the company's shares will

---

*Box 8.1*   Example of pricing a bond new issue.

---

BP is considering the issue of a Eurobond with a 5-year maturity to help fund its operations in America. The company wishes to pay a coupon of 7.5%, or $75 per $1,000 face value (par value). On maturity, the company will return the face value of the bonds to investors.

At present, bonds with similar characteristics and maturity have been issued by a number of oil and gas producers with the same credit rating and business profile as BP. The yield to maturity on these 5-year bonds averages approximately 8%. Thus, 8% is the appropriate discount rate, or yield to maturity, to use in determining the price at which BP's bonds should be issued:

$$\text{Price} = \frac{75}{(1+0.08)^1} + \frac{75}{(1+0.08)^2} + \frac{75}{(1+0.08)^3} + \frac{75}{(1+0.08)^4}$$

$$+ \frac{75}{(1+0.08)^5} + \frac{1,000}{(1+0.08)^5}$$

$$= \frac{75}{(1.08)} + \frac{75}{(1.166)} + \frac{75}{(1.260)} + \frac{75}{(1.360)} + \frac{75}{(1.469)} + \frac{1,000}{(1.469)}$$

$$= 69.444 + 64.322 + 59.524 + 55.147 + 51.055 + 680.735$$

$$= \$980.227$$

Thus, BP would sell bonds with a $1,000 par value at a price of $980.23 per bond. If prevailing interest rates had been lower than 7.5%, the company would have priced its bonds at a level higher than the $1,000 par value.

---

trade. The relative value of a share is its value as determined by the value of a group of similar 'comparable' companies. The market value, sometimes referred to as 'open market value', is defined as the price that an informed willing buyer would pay an informed willing seller for a business or shares of the business.

The value that an analyst comes up with may be very different depending on which method is used. Corporate financiers are most concerned with, in the first place, the intrinsic value of a business. Once she knows the intrinsic value, she will be able to advise her client on most transactions. The intrinsic value of a business is most important when considering a sale or acquisition, while the relative valuation is probably more important when trying to set the price of shares in a flotation or IPO.

Business valuation involves making a great number of assumptions – the ability to construct a complex Excel$^{TM}$ spreadsheet is but one part of the valuation process. Senior corporate financiers use their experience and judgement when determining what method is most appropriate and, once having done so, a plethora of assumptions required to complete the valuation.

This book examines the two most popular corporate valuation approaches: discounted cash flows (based on bond pricing principles) and relative valuations which estimate value by comparing the pricing of comparable companies. In some situations, options-based valuation approaches or asset appraisals may be applied to the valuation of a company's shares. We leave discussion of these to specialist texts, some of which are listed in Additional Reading (p. 223). The technique or techniques chosen and their relative importance will vary from one circumstance to another. Experienced corporate financiers almost always use more than one technique in valuing a company's shares.

# CASH FLOW BASED VALUATIONS

The Discounted Cash Flow (*DCF*) approach to corporate valuation follows the bond valuation approach most closely. However, as noted in the opening paragraphs of the chapter, there is a major difficulty. It is much more difficult to estimate the future cash flows to be generated by a company or one of its divisions than to determine the interest payments on a bond. From a theoretical perspective, DCF valuations provide the most reliable indications of corporate value, but their use is often limited in practice by lack of reliable cash flow forecasts.

The basic steps in determining the value of an enterprise through a DCF valuation are as follows:

- Estimate and analyse future cash flows (frequently derived from earnings projections), ensuring proper adjustment/inclusion for depreciation and amortisation; capital expenditure; changes in working capital.
- Make an estimate of the value of the company (division) following the forecast period (called the *residual* or *terminal value*).
- Determine an appropriate discount rate, to adjust for the time value of money and the riskiness of the cash flows (see Chapter 9).
- Calculate the present value of all future cash flows by application of the discount rate to the estimated cash flows and residual value.

In most instances, a corporate financier will work from forecasts of income statements and balance sheets.

These are accounting presentations. He then needs to determine the economic cash flows that are available to the providers of financing (i.e., debt and equity).

The free cash flow figure computed in a DCF forecast combines information from both the income statement as well as the balance sheet (e.g., capital expenditures are a use of cash, but are not reported on the income statement). Depreciation and amortisation are both recorded as expenses on the income statement, but do not reflect any movement in cash.

Typically, a corporate financier will make a cash flow forecast for a period of 5 years. In particularly volatile or uncertain industries, the forecast period may be only 3 years, while in more stable industries (e.g., utilities) cash flows will be forecast for 10 years or even more in exceptional circumstances. Although it can be difficult, the financial modeller should attempt to capture one business cycle.

For simplicity, our cash flow summary starts with Earnings Before Interest and Tax (*EBIT*) from the income statement (see Box 8.2).

The tax charge represents the taxes that a company would have to pay if it had no debt, marketable securities or non-operating income or expenses. In a free cash flow model the taxes are applied to EBIT at the highest marginal rate.

Free cash flow is the cash that is available to pay a return to the providers of capital – both shareholders and debt-

---

*Box 8.2* Determining free cash flow.

---

**EBIT**

*Less:* Taxes (at highest marginal rate)

*Equals:* Net Operating Profit After Tax (*NOPAT*). This is sometimes referred to as Net Operating Profit Less Adjusted Taxes (*NOPLAT*)

*Plus:* Non-cash expenses; particularly, depreciation and amortisation, etc.

*Less:* Capital expenditure
Increase in working capital

*Note that both these items are found on the balance sheet (and its notes). They are both uses of cash.*

*Equals:* Free cash flow

---

holders. From free cash flow, the corporate financier begins to determine the Enterprise Value of a business – i.e., debt and equity combined.

Table 8.1 illustrates a simplified 5-year forecast of free cash flow, for a business whose EBIT is growing at approximately 6% per annum. When looking at growing businesses – and very few forecasts predict declines – ensure that you also look at the capital expenditure and changes in working capital. Growing businesses almost always need to make capital expenditures and to increase working capital in order to achieve growth.

Once the forecast of free cash flows has been developed, the corporate financier must discount the cash flows by an appropriate discount rate in order to arrive at a present value. Table 8.2 uses the free cash flows from

Table 8.1   Sample cash flow forecast

|  | Year 1 | Year 2 | Year 3 | Year 4 | Year 5 |
|---|---|---|---|---|---|
| EBIT | 100 | 106 | 112 | 119 | 126 |
| Taxes (30%) | 30 | 32 | 34 | 36 | 38 |
| NOPAT | 70 | 74 | 78 | 83 | 88 |
| *Plus:* |  |  |  |  |  |
| Depreciation | 25 | 28 | 30 | 33 | 37 |
| *Less:* |  |  |  |  |  |
| Capital expenditures | 30 | 32 | 33 | 35 | 36 |
| Increase (decrease) in working capital | 12 | 15 | 16 | 10 | (5) |
| **Free cash flow (*FCF*)** | 53 | 55 | 59 | 71 | 94 |

Table 8.1 and a discount rate of 10%. The discount factor (row 2 in Table 8.2) is calculated using the following formula:

$$\frac{1}{(1+r)^n} = \frac{1}{(1.10)^n}$$

The discount factor in row 2 is then multiplied by the

Table 8.2   Determining the DCFs.

| Row | Year 1 | Year 2 | Year 3 | Year 4 | Year 5 |
|---|---|---|---|---|---|
| 1 Free cash flow | 53 | 55 | 59 | 71 | 94 |
| 2 *Times:* Discount factor (10%) | 0.909 | 0.826 | 0.751 | 0.683 | 0.621 |
| 3 PV of FCF | 48 | 45 | 44 | 48 | 58 |
| 4 Total PV of free cash flows | **£243** |  |  |  |  |

free cash flow (row 1) for each year to arrive at the PV of FCF in row 3.

The present value of the forecast cash flows to the enterprise over the next 5 years is £243 million.

# Determination of terminal/residual value

Once the corporate financier has calculated the present value of the cash flows over the forecast period, she is left with the decision of determining the value to be ascribed to the project in the future. In the simplest cases, the final or terminal value of a project is the salvage value of the plant and equipment used. However, when valuing companies or projects with an indeterminate lifespan, a value must be assigned to the business after the end of the explicit cash flow forecast. Often this terminal or residual value can constitute the largest portion of the valuation.

There are three commonly used approaches for determining the terminal value of projects or firms:

- asset value approaches;
- DCF approaches (economic approach);
- relative (or comparable) investment multiples (accounting approach).

### Asset value

In certain project valuation exercises, particularly in the natural resources or extractive industries, the determination of the final value of the project may be relatively easy to determine. The corporate financier simply makes an assumption about the value of the plant and equipment at the end of the project. The value in year 10, say, is then discounted to the present value at the appropriate cost of capital.

### Discounted Cash Flow (economic approach)

The economic approach is the most appropriate method of determining the residual value according to financial theory. We will look at two possibilities. The first assumes there is no further growth in free cash flows following the final year of the forecast. The second assumes continued growth.

The first DCF approach assumes that the final year's free cash flow continues at the same level in perpetuity. The discount rate $(r)$ to be used in the calculation of a perpetual cash flow is the weighted average cost of capital (see Chapter 9). The formula for calculating steady growth for ever is as follows:

$$TV = \frac{CF_n}{r}$$

where  $TV$ = Terminal value or residual value;
 $CF_n$ = Cash flow in final year of forecast $n$;
 $r$ = Discount rate.

Continuing with the prior cash flow example, the final year's cash flow is estimated to be £94 million.

Assuming steady state, the terminal value would be:

$$TV = \frac{94}{0.10}$$

$$= £940 \text{ million}$$

Remember that the £940 million is the estimated value at the end of year 5 – we need to calculate its present value. This is done by multiplying the terminal value (£940 million) by the year 5 present value factor of 0.621 (refer to year 5, row 2 in Table 8.2). The result is a present value of the terminal or residual value of £584 million.

In some instances, a 'steady state' approach is not appropriate. Some companies or projects might legitimately be assumed to continue to grow after the formal forecast period. If the growth is estimated to be a constant, the residual value can be estimated by using the mathematical concept of a growing perpetuity.

The formula for a growing perpetuity is:

$$TV = \frac{CF_n \times (1 + g)}{(r - g)}$$

where   $TV$ = Terminal value;
        $CF_n$ = Cash flow in final year of forecast $n$;
        $r$ = Discount rate;
        $g$ = Growth rate.

It is generally recommended that the maximum growth rate used in the calculation should not exceed the long-term sustainable growth rate of the economy. In companies operating in EU or North American economies, a maximum perpetual growth rate of 2% or 3% would be reasonable.

If the business in our example anticipated its cash flow to grow at 2% per annum in perpetuity, the terminal value would increase to £1,198 million:

$$TV = \frac{94(1.02)}{0.10 - 0.02}$$

$$= \frac{95.88}{0.08}$$

$$= £1,198 \text{ million}$$

Discounting the estimated terminal value to the present using the year 5 discount factor results in a present value of the terminal value of £744 million (£1,198m × 0.621). Note the impact on value of relatively low growth of 2% is significant, even in present value terms. Using a growing perpetuity increases the value of the enterprise by £160 million.

### Relative valuations (accounting approach)

This approach suggests the use of comparable multiples which are fully described in the following section. The corporate financier would find similar companies to the one being valued and take an average of the Price Earnings (PE) multiples. He would then multiply the forecast net income by the PE ratio to estimate the value.

Briefly, assume that in year 5 the net income is forecast to be £94 million and similar companies have a price earnings multiple of 12 times. Multiplying the net profit forecast by the average PE multiple results in a value of £1,128 million. This would then be discounted at the same discount rate, to arrive at an estimate of the equity value of the business of £700 million.

# Determining the discount rate

Chapter 9 addresses the issue of determining the discount rate. In our example, we assume that it is 10%.

# Determining the value of the business

The enterprise value of a business (whether a division, business unit, private or publicly quoted company) is calculated as the sum of the items in Box 8.3.

When cash on hand is valued at its balance sheet amount, it is important that the valuer does not include any investment income from that cash in his cash flow forecast. Redundant assets are assets that the business

---

*Box 8.3* Components of enterprise value.

|   | |
|---|---|
|   | Discounted cash flow (from forecast) |
| + | Present value of terminal value |
| + | Cash on hand at the date of the valuation |
| + | Redundant assets at the date of the valuation |
| = | Enterprise value |

| | Box 8.4   Enterprise valuation. | |
|---|---|---|
| | | **(£m)** |
| | Discounted cash flow | 243 |
| + | Present value of terminal value* | 584 |
| + | Cash on hand** | 3 |
| + | Redundant assets** | — |
| | | |
| | **Enterprise value** | **£830** |

\* Assumes that there is no growth in cash flows beyond the forecast
period and the present value of the perpetual cash flows is used.
\*\*Assumptions made for illustrative purposes.

owns but does not use in its ordinary operations. If they
have value, the assets should be included in enterprise
value calculation.

The enterprise valuation of the example company is
shown in Box 8.4.

*Enterprise value* refers to the value of the assets of the
business. (Here the business can be a division of a company, a privately held company, a stock exchange listed
company or other entity.) The assets do not refer to the
accounting book value or to the salvage value. It is the
present value of the cash flows the assets of the firm are
capable of generating. Enterprise value does not concern
itself with how the assets are financed.

The value of the equity in the business is simply the
enterprise value less the market value of outstanding
debt, preference shares or other forms of financing.
Lenders and preference shareholders have a prior claim

Box 8.5 Calculation of equity value.

Discounted cash flow:
+ Present value of terminal value
+ Cash on hand
+ Redundant assets
= Enterprise value

Less:

Market value of preference shares
Market value of debt

= **Equity value**

on the assets of a company, ahead of ordinary share-holders. Therefore, the equity value of the business is the residual of the enterprise value after deduction for prior claims.

In practice, it can be difficult to determine the market value of the debt and other securities. When this is the case, corporate financiers tend to use the book value.

For example, the company has £325 million face value in long-term debt, but the market value is £300 million. Therefore, £300 million is subtracted from the enter-prise value to determine the equity value. There are no preference shares outstanding, as shown in Box 8.6.

The equity value is the estimate of the business's market capitalisation. Note that while the discounted cash flow valuation approach is the most 'scientific', it does suffer from shortcomings. In particular, there are estimation errors surrounding most cash flow forecasts,

Box 8.6   Calculation of equity value.

| | | (£m) |
|---|---|---:|
| | Discounted cash flow | 243 |
| + | Present value of terminal value* | 584 |
| + | Cash on hand** | 3 |
| + | Redundant assets** | — |
| | Enterprise value | 830 |
| *Less*: | | |
| | Market value of preference shares | — |
| | Market value of debt** | 300 |
| = | **Equity value** | **£530** |

\* Assumes that there is no growth in cash flows beyond the forecast period and the present value of the perpetual cash flows is used.
\*\*Assumptions made for illustrative purposes.

determination of the terminal value and, often most importantly, the choice of discount rate.

Most corporate financiers use the DCF approach in conjunction with another valuation method. In particular, they use investment ratios (multiples) from comparable companies (see the Appendix).

# RELATIVE VALUATIONS

The most common, and in many ways the easiest to complete, method of valuing a company's equity is by comparing a number of financial and investment ratios with those of the firm's peer group. In general, it is easy to calculate multiples for other companies and they are particularly useful when there are a large number of comparable firms being traded, and the market is pricing these firms correctly.

However, the determination of what is a 'comparable' is not always straightforward and is often open to interpretation. Some of the key areas of difference and, therefore, difficulty in selecting companies as comparables include:

- size and future growth prospects of the company;
- riskiness of the business;
- scope of product offerings;
- variance in customer base;
- geographic reach;
- current and future profitability.

All these factors have an impact on the valuation of comparable companies, and judgement needs to be made in drawing conclusions as to the appropriate multiples to be used for the value range.

In some instances, particularly when comparing a privately held company with the investment ratios of public companies, adjustments must be made. The most frequent adjustments are:

To reported earnings:

- elimination of one-off items;
- add back 'excessive' management remuneration to EBIT;
- adjustments to align accounting policies with those used by public companies.

To multiples:

- a discount to compensate for the non-marketability of private company shares;
- a premium for control;
- an adjustment to reflect variations in overall quality of earnings (i.e., earnings variability).

## Price earnings ratio

The most common earnings valuation method is the Price Earnings Ratio (*PER* or *PE ratio*) which is the multiple that the price or value represents of annual maintainable earnings. The earnings figures used are those earnings attributable to ordinary shareholders after deductions for interest, tax, minority interest and dividends attributable to preference shareholders.

The PE multiple (or ratio) is calculated as the market price per share divided by earnings per share. An alternative approach to the method is to take the market capitalisation of the company divided by net earnings (or profit or income) after tax. The resulting multiple will be identical.

As a simple example, consider a company with earnings attributable to ordinary shareholders of £5 million. A corporate financier who believes that a PE multiple of between 8 and 12 is appropriate would value the company at between £40 million and £60 million. If the company had 10 million shares outstanding, the earnings per share would be 50p. Applying a multiple of between 8 and 12 times would result in an estimated share price of 400p to 600p. This is often referred to as the capitalisation of earnings approach to valuation.

## Price/EBIT multiple

An alternative earnings valuation method is to use a multiple of a business's earnings before interest and taxation (i.e., market capitalisation divided by EBIT). EBIT multiples are not commonly quoted for public companies, but are of particular use for situations where a stand-alone business is being acquired, and/or where the business being valued is highly leveraged.

## Market to book value

The market to book value ratio, also called the *price to book value ratio*, is another frequently examined ratio. The market value of a company's shares (i.e., price) is divided by its book value per share; alternatively, the market capitalisation of a company is divided by the firm's shareholders' funds. Its importance is greater in some sectors (e.g., banking) than others (e.g., high-tech, software).

Some analysts favour the ratio because the book value is a relative constant which eases comparability over time or across companies. The price to book value ratio can be calculated even when a company's earnings or EBIT are negative. However, the book value does not reflect the assets' earning power and projected cash flows. It reflects the assets' original cost and is affected by accounting decisions on depreciation. Finally, the ratio is not very useful in valuing service firms without significant fixed assets.

# Dividend yield

The dividend yield valuation model is infrequently used, but when it is used, it is those businesses with a steady level of profitability and a consistent payout of a large proportion of earnings in the form of dividends that are the most appropriate subjects. It also can be used for the valuation of minority shareholdings. This technique values the dividend stream by comparing it with that available from other securities.

To calculate the equity value it is necessary to divide the dividend paid by the appropriate dividend yield. The appropriate dividend yield is chosen by reference to the Stock Market, to private transactions or to dividend yields on comparable businesses. By way of example, assume that similar firms to ours have an average prospective dividend yield (i.e., next year's estimated dividend per share divided by today's share price) of 3%. If we anticipate the payment of £25 million in dividends next year, we can estimate the firm's equity value:

$$\text{Equity value} = \frac{\text{Expected dividend}}{\text{Prospective dividend yield}}$$

$$= \frac{\text{£25m}}{3\%}$$

$$= \text{£833 million}$$

There are potential pitfalls when valuing on a dividend basis. First, the certainty of the dividend stream must be assessed both in terms of dividend policy where the shareholding does not give control, and in terms of the stability of earnings. Second, an assessment must be made of the proportion of earnings paid out as dividends ('the payout ratio') for it may be misleading to apply a dividend yield derived from companies with low-payout ratios to the dividend paid out by companies with high-payout ratios.

## Enterprise value to EBITDA

This ratio first gained widespread use in the mid-1990s and continues to be popular. Enterprise value is calculated as:

Market capitalisation

$$= \frac{\text{Number of shares outstanding}}{\text{Share price}}$$
$$+ \text{Market value of outstanding debt}$$

The multiple compares the enterprise value of the business with its Earnings Before Interest, Tax, Depreciation and Amortisation ($EBITDA$) which is essentially an alternative measure of cash flow.

EBITDA is seen as a proxy for cash flow and is a useful number to use, particularly in companies or industries that are growing rapidly and may have not yet achieved profitability. The benefits of the ratio are numerous. It may be computed for firms that have net losses and can be more appropriate for industries which require a substantial investment in infrastructure and long gestation periods (e.g., new telcos). For LBO (highly levered) transactions, EBITDA multiples capture the ability of the firm to generate cash flows that may be used to support debt payments in the short run. Finally, the EBITDA multiple allows for comparison of firms with different financial leverage.

## Determining the value of a business based on ratios/multiples

In this section we examine the financial results of a privately held manufacturer, 'Blockade Holdings' and compare it with publicly traded companies in order to determine a valuation range for the company. Table 8.3 contains selected valuation statistics for five similar manufacturing companies. A corporate financier has assessed each of these business and deems them to be similar in size, product line, extent of operations, major accounting policies, etc.

In this table, EV refers to Enterprise Value (the sum of the firms' market capitalisation and market value of its outstanding debt). Price refers either to share price or to market capitalisation of the firm's equity.

Note that the mean and median statistics are fairly close for most ratios. This indicates that for most ratios there is not a company with outlying results, which may skew the valuation range. The exception to this is column 8,

Table 8.3  Publicly traded comparables.

| 1 | 2 | 3 | 4 | 5 | 6 | 7 | 8 | 9 | 10 | 11 | 12 |
|---|---|---|---|---|---|---|---|---|---|---|---|
| Company | Price (p) | Market capital- isation (bn) | 1-year return | PER 2005 | PER 2006 | EV/ EBITDA | Price/ FCF | Market capital- isation/ book value | EV/ Revenues | EBITDA/ Revenues | Dividend yield |
| Lawrence | 479 | £26.4 | 38% | 18.7 | 14.3 | 6.9 | 26.2 | 1.00 | 1.24 | 18% | 3.5% |
| Wilson | 216 | £1.1 | NA | 14.4 | 13.5 | 7.3 | 12.9 | 0.16 | 0.64 | 9% | 1.7% |
| Hodges | 378 | £3.3 | 27% | 7.6 | 7.1 | 4.5 | 16 | 0.55 | 0.70 | 16% | 4.6% |
| Ranson | 53 | £0.6 | −36% | 11.8 | 7.3 | 3.9 | 14.5 | 0.25 | 0.51 | 13% | 5.7% |
| Allen | 773 | £5.8 | 46% | 13.8 | 12.7 | 6.6 | −138.1 | 0.79 | 1.01 | 15% | 3.1% |
| Average | | | | 13.3 | 11.0 | 5.8 | −13.7 | 0.55 | 0.82 | 14% | 3.7% |
| Median | | | | 13.8 | 12.7 | 6.6 | 14.5 | 0.55 | 0.70 | 15% | 4.0% |
| Minimum | | | | 7.6 | 7.1 | 3.9 | −138.1 | 0.2 | 0.51 | 9% | 1.7% |
| Maximum | | | | 18.7 | 14.3 | 7.3 | 26.2 | 1.0 | 1.24 | 18% | 5.7% |

Box 8.7   Blockade Holdings summary financial statements.

| Income statement | 2005 (£m) |
| --- | --- |
| Revenues | 300 |
| EBITDA | 50 |
| Depreciation | 14 |
| EBIT | 36 |
| Interest expense | 12 |
| Earnings before tax | 24 |
| Income tax | 7 |
| Profit after tax | 17 |
| Dividends | 7 |
| Free cash flow | 12 |

| Summary balance sheet | Year end 2005 (£m) |
| --- | --- |
| Fixed assets | 400 |
| Current assets | 100 |
| Current liabilities | 60 |
| Long-term debt | 80 |
| Shareholders' equity | 360 |

the Price/Free Cash Flow (*FCF*) column (market capitalisation of equity divided by free cash flow). Allen has a negative FCF, which adversely affects the average of the five companies. Ignoring Allen gives an average Price/FCF of 17.4 and a median of 15.3 for the remaining four companies. Box 8.7 contains summary financial results for the company.

The company's profit after tax is expected to grow to £20 million in the following year (2006) from £17 million in 2005. FCF for the year has been estimated as £12 million, reflecting capital expenditure and increases in working capital to finance the company's growth.

Table 8.4 contains the workings of the summary comparable valuation for Blockade Holdings. The mean and the median multiples from Table 8.3 are in the second column from the left (*Comparable multiple*). In the third

*Table 8.4*  Comparables-based valuation.

| Ratio | Comparable multiple | | Amount | Equity value range | |
|---|---|---|---|---|---|
| | Average value | Median value | | (based on average) | (based on median) |
| | (£m) | (£m) | (£m) | (£m) | (£m) |
| Earnings (trailing 2005) | 13 | 14 | 17 | 226 | 235 |
| Earnings 2006 est. | 11 | 12.7 | 20 | 220 | 254 |
| Free cash flow | 15.3 | 17.4 | 12 | 184 | 209 |
| Dividend yield | 0.035 | 0.037 | 7 | 200 | 189 |
| Book value (NAV) | 0.55 | 0.55 | 360 | 198 | 198 |
| EBITDA (as adjusted below) | | | | 210 | 250 |
| Revenues (as adjusted below) | | | | 130 | 166 |
| Range | | | | 130 | 250 |
| Median of midpoints | | | | **198** | |
| Mean of midpoints | | | | **205** | |
| | | | | **Enterprise value** | |
| EV/EBITDA | 5.8 | 6.6 | 50 | 290 | 330 |
| EV/Revenue | 0.70 | 0.82 | 300 | 210 | 246 |

column (*Amount*) is the comparable figure from Blockade's financial statements as presented in Box 8.7. Our analysis (done elsewhere) has shown that the company's operating and financial characteristics are average when compared with the comparable group. The second column is multiplied by the third column to get the equity or enterprise valuation based on that multiple.

The column *Comparable multiple* contains a range of values based on the median and mean of the comparable companies as presented in Table 8.4. *Amount* is the figure for Blockade – e.g., in the 'Earnings (trailing 2005)' row we insert Blockade's net profit of £17 million. The 'Equity value range' column is the product of the two columns to its left – *Comparable multiple* multiplied by *Amount*.

Therefore, assuming we have chosen appropriate comparables, the market capitalisation of Blockade should be between £226 million and £235 million, based on an earnings multiple. Corporate financiers will always look at numerous multiples when arriving at an estimate of value.

In order to adjust the enterprise valuation to make it comparable with the equity valuation, subtract the value of debt (£80 million). In this example, we assume that the book value of the debt is the same as its market value as we do not have access to market figures.

Therefore, the equity value based on the EV/EBITDA multiple of 5.8 is £210 million (an enterprise value of £290 million less £80 million of outstanding debt), and the equity value based on EV/Revenues is £145 million (enterprise value of £225m less the value of debt, £80 million).

Based on the figures (median £198 million and mean £205 million) the management of Blockade would probably set the value of the business at approximately £200 million. A reasonable range for the valuation of the equity of the business, based on this extremely limited information, would be from, say, £185 million to, say, £215 million. Note that this final range has been called reasonable. It is based on the author's judgement: something that is very important in all valuations. Although the use of formulas and numerical ratios make valuation appear to be a science, it remains very much an art.

# Chapter

# 9

DETERMINING THE
COST OF CAPITAL

The previous chapter introduced the DCF approach to company valuation. We noted that the approach was the most scientific, but suffered from limitations – in particular, the accuracy of cash flow forecasts. A second issue affecting the accuracy of DCF valuations is the selection of an appropriate rate at which to discount the cash flows.

The discount rate that is to be used is the firm's 'cost of capital'; that is, the amount (in percent) that the firm must 'pay' to its providers of capital. In Chapter 2 we discussed the various sources of capital available to corporations, from commercial paper, to convertible bonds to ordinary shares. Each source of capital has a cost – some higher than others. Corporate financiers work with their clients to minimise the firm's cost of capital because as the discount rate declines the firm's value increases.

In this chapter we will focus on the costs of the two main sources of capital: debt and equity.

# WEIGHTED AVERAGE COST OF CAPITAL

When trying to determine the correct discount rate, corporate financiers calculate a weighted average of the cost of each component or source of finance (capital). The Weighted Average Cost of Capital (WACC) is also known as the opportunity cost of capital (i.e., the amount of return that a rational investor requires for an investment of similar risk).

The WACC is calculated on an after-tax basis, since free cash flows represent cash available to all providers of capital. Remember when calculating free cash flows we deduct a notional tax charge from the Earnings Before Interest and Tax (*EBIT*) to determine Net Operating Profit After Tax (*NOPAT*).

The formula for the WACC of a company with two sources of capital is set out below:

$$WACC = [(K_d \times (1 - t)) \times (D/T)] + [K_e \times (E/T)]$$

where  $K_d$ = Cost of debt;
       $t$ = Tax rate;
       $D$ = Total debt (market value);
       $E$ = Total equity (market value);
       $T$ = Debt + Equity (market values);
       $K_e$ = Cost of equity.

There are four rules that corporate financiers should obey when calculating the WACC in corporate valuation.

## Use market values

The weights used in the formula should be based on the market values of debt and equity, not their book values. The WACC is the expected return on a firm's securities based on their current price – i.e., the return a new investor would require before purchasing the bonds or shares.

Given this definition, it is clear that the book or accounting values of debt and equity are not appropriate in the weighting. New investors cannot buy shares at book value – they must pay the market price. Similarly, investors in corporate bonds or corporate loans will receive a return that has been adjusted by the market to reflect current market conditions, investment risk, income (interest rate paid) and maturity of the bonds.

However, it is often impossible to determine the market value of privately held debt. When this is the case, the corporate financier is forced to use the book value in her calculation.

## Use target/optimal weighting

The proportions used in the WACC are the expected or target proportions of debt and equity capital intended to finance the company during the period in question. Raising capital is 'chunky'. Companies typically wait until they require a significant sum and then raise capital either through the debt or equity capital markets or via a bank loan. Thus, they will regularly deviate from their targets. This should not be seen as an issue as long as, over time, companies tend to stay near their target ratios.

Changes in market prices will also change the existing ratios of debt to equity and other financing sources on a daily basis. It is more appropriate to use the company's long-term target capital structure.

When determining the target capital structure, the corporate financier will estimate the current market value based capital structure of the company. He then reviews the capital structure of other companies. Finally, the management's approach to financing the business and its implications for the target capital structure is reviewed and an appropriate capital structure is set.

## After tax

The WACC must be stated after tax, as free cash flow is also stated after tax. Remember that the free cash flows that are being discounted are based on NOPAT plus depreciation less capital expenditures and increases in working capital.

## Match nominal rates with nominal cash flows

In general, nominal rates of return (or costs) should be used. This matches the nominal cash flows that are used in the free cash flow forecast.

In highly inflationary environments, one may wish to calculate a 'real' discount rate to discount 'real' cash flows. This is because high inflation rates are often very volatile and the forecaster's accuracy can be thrown off. The key rule to remember is that the analyst should never mix nominal cash flows with real discount rates and *vice versa*.

---

*Box 9.1*   Example.

---

Company X has the following costs of capital:

| | |
|---|---|
| Cost of debt (pre-tax) | 8% |
| Cost of equity | 11% |
| Tax rate | 30% |
| Market value of debt | €5m |
| Book value of debt | €5m |
| Market value of equity | €20m |
| Book value of equity | €10m |

The WACC is determined as follows: First, determine the after-tax cost of debt:

$$8\% \times (1 - 30\%) = 8\% \times (0.70) = 5.6\%$$

Second, using market values, determine the total capital outstanding:

$$€5 + €20 = €25 \text{ million}$$

Third, determine the portions of debt and equity:

$$\text{Debt}\left(\frac{D}{T}\right) = \frac{€5}{€25} = 0.20$$

$$\text{Equity}\left(\frac{E}{T}\right) = \frac{€20}{€25} = 0.80$$

Fourth, fill in the equation to determine the WACC:

$$WACC = \left[ (K_d \times (1 - t)) \times \frac{D}{T} \right] + \left[ K_e \times \frac{E}{T} \right]$$

$$= [(8.0 \times (1 - 0.3)) \times 0.20] + [11 \times 0.80]$$

$$= [5.6 \times 0.20] + [11 \times 0.80]$$

$$= 1.12 + 8.80$$

$$= 9.92\%$$

# COST OF DEBT: $K_d$

The cost of debt to a company is the borrowing cost that the company would pay if it was raising funds today. It is not the existing coupon on its bonds and debentures. It must be stated after tax in order to match the cash flows which are also stated after tax.

There are two approaches to determining the cost of debt:

1. Calculate the yield to maturity and current market values of all outstanding debt. With this information, determine the WACC.
2. Estimate the cost of debt using the 'debt risk premium' method.

The cost of debt is not the coupon rate. It is the current yield to maturity: the opportunity cost of debt.

The first method is the most appropriate, but only works if the business has issued debt for which current yields to maturity can be determined. So, if a firm has issued bonds with a coupon of 9% and a current yield to maturity of 7.5%, the latter figure would be used in calculating the cost of debt. Remember also that if the yield to maturity has changed from the initial coupon rate, the market price of the bonds will also have changed. If the yield to maturity has increased, the market price of the bonds will be lower than the initial book price, while if the yield to maturity has decreased, the market price of the bonds will have increased.

The debt risk premium method is less exact and less preferred by finance professionals. The corporate financier first finds the risk-free rate (a government bond) and adds a premium for the risk of the company. Typically, the corporate financier will find the credit rating of the company from one of the credit rating agencies and apply the appropriate premium over the government bond.

# COST OF EQUITY: $K_e$

As noted above, the calculation of the cost of debt for companies with publicly traded fixed income securities is fairly straightforward. The calculation of the cost of equity, for both public and private companies, is more difficult.

Remember from the above sections that a company's cost of capital is the same figure as investors' expected returns from investing in that company's securities.

When estimating the cost of equity or the expected return on equity, the corporate financier needs to estimate the present value of future dividends as well as the present value of the share's anticipated capital appreciation.

In the past, corporate financiers commonly used the dividend discount model to determine the firm's cost of equity. The dividend discount model is a rearrangement of the equation used in the dividend yield approach to valuation. The formula follows:

$$K_e = \frac{\text{Div}_1}{P_0} + g$$

where $K_e$ = Cost of equity;
$\text{Div}_1$ = Dividend per share expected to be paid in the next year;
$P_0$ = Price per share today;
$g$ = Growth rate of dividends in percent per annum.

---

*Box 9.2* Example.

---

In October 2005, HSBC – the international banking group – had a share price of 920p and a dividend per share in the past 12 months of 37p per share. Stock Market analysts predicted that its dividend would increase to 41p per share in 2001 and maintain long-term growth of 4%.

According to the dividend model, HSBC's cost of equity at that time was:

$$K_e = \frac{41}{920} + 4.0\%$$

$$= 0.0444 + 0.04$$

$$= 0.0844$$

$$= 8.44\%$$

Clearly, the dividend model has limitations in its ability to predict the cost of equity: it cannot calculate a cost for companies that do not pay any dividends, nor can it deal with variable dividend growth rates.

# CAPITAL ASSET PRICING MODEL

During the 1980s, an academic model that had been developed in the 1960s, called the *Capital Asset Pricing Model (CAPM)* began to gain popularity among corporate financiers. The CAPM (pronounced 'cap-em') is a theory of the relationship between the risk of an asset (company) and the expected rate of return required on the asset.

The opportunity cost of capital equals the return on a risk-free asset plus the company's systematic risk (beta) times the market price of risk (market risk premium). The formula, originally derived for investment management purposes, is as follows:

$$K_e = r_f + \beta(r_m - r_f)$$

where  $K_e$ = Cost of equity or expected return;
$r_f$ = Risk-free rate of return;
$\beta$ = Beta;
$r_m$ = (Expected) equity market return;
$(r_m - r_f)$ = Equity risk premium.

The CAPM begins by assuming that investors require a return of at least that which can be earned on the risk-free asset (i.e., the risk-free return). Its next step says that to be attracted to investing in the stock market, an investor requires a premium to compensate him for the additional risk involved. This is represented as $(r_m - r_f)$ and is referred to as the *equity risk premium* or *market premium*.

The major (simplifying) assumption of the CAPM is that the only influence on a share price movement is the movement of the stock market as a whole (market risk). Thus, CAPM finds that the risk of an individual company's share is found in its beta factor. Beta is a measure of a share's riskiness compared with the stock market as a whole.

You should note that the above paragraph is a gross simplification of the theory supporting the CAPM. Those readers who are interested should consult any finance textbook – Brealey and Myers (2000) is a good one. For those corporate financiers who are really keen, the original theory is set out in three papers authored by Sharpe (1964), Lintner (1965) and Treynor (1965).

The following sections examine each component of the CAPM in greater detail.

# Risk-free rate

The risk-free rate is the return on a security that has no default risk. Theoretically, any government security in the home market (e.g., Gilts for valuing UK companies) can be used. For company valuation medium- to long-term government bonds are used to determine the risk-free rate. The most popular is the yield to maturity on the 10-year Gilt. Short-term rates such as the 3-month Treasury Bill are not used as they are strongly influenced by short-term inflation considerations.

# Market risk premium (equity risk premium)

The market risk premium is the difference between the expected rate of return on the market portfolio and the risk-free rate. Historically determined risk premia can be used (and frequently are), as the long-term relationship between the stock market's returns and the risk-free return is relatively stable. Note that the short-term relationship – i.e., less than 10 years – can vary significantly.

In both the UK and the US, 4.0–5.0% above the government bond rate is typically used as the 'equity risk premium' (see the Appendix for a survey of UK corporate financiers' usage).

# Beta $(\beta)$

The beta measures the extent to which the returns on a given stock move with a market index. It is a measure of relative risk.

A beta of 1 means that a company's shares are expected to move in line with the market. A beta of 1.5 means that if the index changes by 1.0%, the stock will change price by 1.5% in the same direction as the market. The beta reflects both industry- and company-specific factors.

Companies that are riskier than the overall equity market have a beta greater than 1, while those that are less risky have a beta of less than 1. The beta for most companies falls within the range of 0.6 and 1.5.

---

*Box 9.3* Example.

In October 2005, the 10-year gilt yield (UK Government Bond) was approximately 4.75% and HSBC's beta was 0.95, reflecting the relatively low variability of its shares compared with the market. Assuming that the equity risk premium for the UK was 4%, HSBC's cost of equity was:

$$K_e = 4.75 + 0.95(4.0)$$

$$= 4.75 + 3.80$$

$$= 8.55\%$$

---

# Health warning

The corporate financier should note that there are significant problems with using the CAPM to determine the cost of equity of a business. Academic studies in many countries have found that the beta factor is not a good predictor of security returns. However, the formula continues to be employed by most corporate financiers in the UK because of its ease of use and the lack of any widely accepted substitute.

# Chapter

# 10

....................................................

# SHAREHOLDER VALUE ADDED

## (Economic profit)

One of the most important developments in corporate finance during the 1990s was the rediscovery of the concept of economic profit developed by an English economist, Alfred Marshall, in the 1890s. Economic profit evaluates a firm's, division's or business unit's financial performance over a specific time period. A firm with positive economic profit is creating value for its shareholders. Negative economic profit destroys value: shareholders would be better off making an alternative investment.

Economic profit travels under many guises, depending on which firm of consultants you are talking to. The most widespread term is EVA$^{TM}$ which is the acronym for Economic Value Added. Others use Shareholder Value Added (*SVA*) or Cash Flow Return on Investment (*CFROI*).

## JUST ANOTHER NUMBER?

Accounting profit is the figure struck after all expenses and taxes are deducted from the firm's revenues during the period under evaluation. These expenses include interest paid to the holders of the firm's debt obligations (bankers and bondholders). However, there is no explicit treatment of returns to shareholders – i.e., what is the cost of equity?

Another shortcoming of financial accounting performance figures is that they do not incorporate a figure for risk. Thus, senior management is not able to discern whether a project's performance has delivered a return that is commensurate with its risk.

Thus, traditional measures, using accounting data, have been found to be poor predictors of future shareholder returns. Companies with a value maximisation objective desire internal measures for evaluating strategic initiatives and ongoing performance which provide an accurate reflection of value creation. Many firms have adopted shareholder value measures for internal use because they have been found to be a more accurate predictor of shareholder returns than accounting measures.

The measurement combines a firm's financial return, capital used in generating the return and a measure of the firm's risk in a single figure. Economic profit uses the same tools as those employed in a discounted cash flow valuation: cash flows (not accounting profit), cash invested in the business and the Weighted Average Cost of Capital ($WACC$).

Accounting measures typically evaluate only one or sometimes two of the above, but never all three. For example, return on equity and Return On Capital Employed ($ROCE$) use data from both the income statement and balance sheet – however, they do not take account of the project's or business's risk.

## BENEFITS OF SVA

The SVA approach is consistent with investors' views of drivers of shareholder returns. Investors understand that a company or project must earn a return in excess of its cost of capital (risk) in order to create value for the suppliers of capital. It is academically sound, being based on Discounted Cash Flows (*DCFs*) and WACC. In addition, studies indicate there is a greater correlation between shareholder return and SVA measures than there is between shareholder return and traditional accounting measures including earnings per share, return on equity and others.

It is easily understood by managers and will influence operational decisions to enhance value. Managers can invest in high-return projects, reduce the amount of capital devoted to low-return projects or reduce the cost of capital. It also makes the cost of capital clearly visible to managers. Many operating managers are unaware of the concept of cost of capital. By using SVA with its capital charge, senior management are able to 'monetise' the cost of capital and ensure that managers seek to minimise the capital used.

SVA provides a single figure for financial performance allowing management to concentrate on a single monetary figure in determination of performance. Many companies use SVA in the financial portion of a balanced scorecard assessment programme.

Finally, it is easy to measure and implement. The SVA calculation is relatively straightforward and can be employed at both business unit and corporate levels.

Many companies have adopted measures like this to judge their performance internally, across business units and with their peer group. Prominent examples include Coca-Cola, Boots, LloydsTSB and VEBA.

# CALCULATION OF SVA

SVA is a single period performance measure of whether a business has created or destroyed value. Put simply, a firm creates value when its ROCE is greater than its cost of capital. ROCE is a function of *Net Operating Profit After Tax (NOPAT)* and invested capital, while the cost of capital is determined by the return expected by the market – i.e., WACC.

NOPAT measures return by adjusting operating profit for corporation tax. The NOPAT figure used in economic profit calculation is the same figure as derived in the DCF valuations introduced in Chapter 8 (Box 8.2). NOPAT is the pre-interest, post-tax operating profit earned by the company or business unit.

Capital employed or invested capital is the amount of resources required to generate the return. In the following simple examples, we define invested capital as shareholders' funds plus total debt (both long-term and short-term). For simplicity of calculation, the examples in this book use the book value of shareholders' funds.

Some approaches to SVA (notably EVA and CFROI) make several adjustments to invested capital to more accurately reflect the current value of assets and to take account of certain items that are often expensed on an income statement, but have a useful life of more than

1 year. One of the main items that is typically expensed is Research and Development (R&D), but the value of R&D done in 1 year often continues for many years.

The cost of capital is the measure of the required return by investors in the company's debt and equity securities. It is the weighted average of the cost of debt financing and equity finance used by the company, or allocated to the division/business unit. The cost of capital incorporates a measure of the risk of the business. Businesses operating in higher risk sectors of the economy will have higher costs of capital. Similarly, businesses with an excessive amount of debt in their capital structure will be punished by the capital markets with a higher cost of capital.

Table 10.1 presents the summary income statement and balance sheet for a fictitious company.

There are two ways to calculate the economic profit of a company. Both are valid and will arrive at the same figure. One is called the *spread* method and the other the *capital charge* method (Table 10.2).

Table 10.3 illustrates the calculation of economic profit using the spread method. It starts by calculating the NOPAT for each of the 5 years ended December 2001 to 2005. NOPAT is divided by the opening capital (i.e., invested capital at the end of the prior year). The opening capital for 2003 is £372 million (the capital on the balance sheet at 31 December 2002). The capital employed calculation can be based on opening capital (as in this example), average capital employed during the

*Table 10.1*   Example of economic profit calculation.

| | Summary balance sheet | | | | | |
| | Opening | 2001 | 2002 | 2003 | 2004 | 2005 |
|---|---|---|---|---|---|---|
| Working capital | 0 | 33 | 41 | 48 | 55 | 54 |
| Fixed assets | 300 | 315 | 331 | 347 | 365 | 383 |
| Net assets | 300 | 348 | 372 | 395 | 420 | 437 |
| Net debt | 150 | 164 | 155 | 136 | 113 | 68 |
| Equity | 150 | 184 | 217 | 259 | 307 | 369 |
| Total capital | 300 | 348 | 372 | 395 | 420 | 437 |
| | Summary – profit and loss | | | | | |
| Revenue | | 250 | 275 | 303 | 333 | 366 |
| Cost of sales | | 125 | 137 | 152 | 166 | 183 |
| Gross profit | | 125 | 138 | 151 | 167 | 183 |
| Other expenses | | 50 | 50 | 75 | 75 | 75 |
| EBIT | | 75 | 88 | 76 | 92 | 108 |
| Interest expense | | 24 | 23 | 21 | 18 | 13 |
| Earnings before tax | | 51 | 65 | 55 | 74 | 95 |
| Taxation | | 18 | 23 | 19 | 26 | 33 |
| Net profit after tax | | 33 | 42 | 36 | 48 | 62 |

year or on closing capital. The important thing is to remain consistent throughout the analysis.

It has been determined that this business has a WACC of 10%.

In 2001, NOPAT of £52 is divided by opening capital of £300, resulting in an ROCE of 17.3%. As the 17.3%

*Table 10.2*  Calculating economic profit.

| Capital charge method | | Spread method | |
|---|---|---|---|
| | NOPAT (£) | | ROCE (%) |
| *less*: | (Capital employed (%) × WACC (%)) | *less*: | WACC (%) |
| *equals*: | Economic Profit (SVA) (£) | *equals*: | Spread |
| | | *times*: | Capital Employed (£) |
| | | *equals*: | Economic Profit (SVA) (£) |

*Table 10.3*  Calculation of SVA using Spread Method

| | 2001 | 2002 | 2003 | 2004 | 2005 |
|---|---|---|---|---|---|
| EBIT | 75 | 88 | 76 | 92 | 108 |
| Tax (30%) | 23 | 26 | 23 | 27 | 32 |
| NOPAT | 52 | 62 | 53 | 65 | 76 |
| Opening capital employed | 300 | 348 | 372 | 395 | 420 |
| ROCE | 17.3% | 17.8% | 14.2% | 16.4% | 18.1% |
| *less*:    WACC | 10.0% | 10.0% | 10.0% | 10.0% | 10.0% |
| *equals*: Spread | 7.3% | 7.8% | 4.2% | 6.4% | 8.1% |
| *times*: Opening capital employed | 300 | 348 | 372 | 395 | 420 |
| *equals*: SVA | 22 | 27 | 16 | 25 | 34 |

ROCE exceeds the firm's cost of capital, we know that the company has created value for its shareholders.

The 'spread' is determined by subtracting the WACC from the ROCE, resulting in a 7.3% spread for the company (17.3% − 10% = 7.3%).

To determine just how much shareholder value has been created, the final step is to determine the SVA by multiplying the invested capital (£300 million) by the spread (7.3%). This results in SVA of £22 million.

# Limitations of economic profit calculations

Using balance sheet figures to calculate invested capital can distort the economic profit calculation. The balance sheet is comprised of items recorded at their time of purchase or periodic revaluation, thus it is based on historic costs. Fixed assets and some intangible assets are depreciated over time which will often lead to an understatement of their true economic value on a balance sheet. If an analyst relies solely on historic balance sheet figures to determine the invested capital, the figure for invested capital will be lower than otherwise expected, leading to a higher economic profit than deserved by the company or division.

For this reason, adjustments are made (up to 164 in the case of EVA), which leads to a second potential shortcoming in the calculation of economic profit. Wherever adjustments are made, they depend in part on the judgement of the manager or analyst involved.

Certain projects – particularly in their early, high-growth, high-investment stages – may result in a negative economic profit. This is in spite of a potentially high net present value over the life of the project. Managers must be warned against excessive reliance and short-termism in their analysis of economic profit figures and ensuing actions.

# Appendix

. . . . . . . . . . . . . . . . . . . . . . . . . . . . . . . . . . . . . . .

# UK CORPORATE VALUATION METHODS: A SURVEY

This appendix presents the results of a survey of experienced corporate finance practitioners in the UK and Ireland conducted in May and June 1998. Questionnaires were sent to 452 corporate finance directors at 71 banks, stock brokers, venture capitalists and accountancy firms listed in *Crawford's Directory*. A total of 113 usable responses were returned from 41 different firms by the 14 July 1998 cut-off date. This represents a response rate of 25.0% of individuals and 57.7% of firms surveyed.

Although the survey was conducted a number of years ago, its results continue to be broadly valid, with the possible exceptions of the current perceived equity risk premium and the usage of the Internet to research companies.

## Scoring and tables

Most questions required a response regarding the frequency of use of a method or source of information. The scale used is as follows:

| 1 | 2 | 3 | 4 | 5 |
|---|---|---|---|---|
| Almost never | Seldom | Some-times | Usually | Almost always |
| 0–5% | 6–35% | 36–65% | 66–95% | 96–100% |

The tables in this report contain the mean score, standard deviation and the percentage of each respondent selecting 1, 2, 3, 4 or 5. Percentages may not add to

100% because of rounding and, in some cases, multiple responses.

# A.1  VALUATION METHODOLOGY

There are two main approaches to determining the value of a company:

- relative valuation techniques; *and*
- determination of intrinsic or 'true' value.

UK corporate finance professionals use relative valuation techniques most often. This may reflect the ease with which, in most cases, comparable companies can be found. However, numerous limitations affect the reliability of sole reliance on comparable methods. These include differences in accounting policies; identification of suitable companies; hidden assets and liabilities; and non-overlapping ranges; but ignores synergies in the case of an acquisition.

Possibly the most important concern relating to relative valuation methods is when most or all companies are trading at levels above their intrinsic value (a speculative bubble). Certain acquisitions or flotations may be attractive on a relative basis, but cannot be justified on the basis of intrinsic value.

Determination of 'intrinsic' value is generally accomplished through the application of Discounted Cash Flow (*DCF*) techniques. This method was ranked sixth in terms of frequency of use, but as one of the two most important methods as detailed in Table A.2.

DCF approaches also suffer from limitations: identification of forecast cash flows can be difficult if the corporate financier does not have access to management forecasts and the calculation of an appropriate discount rate is subject to debate. The ability to achieve arithmetically precise valuations using computer spreadsheets can also seduce the inexperienced into believing that DCF valuations are more accurate. As many financiers noted: 'valuation is as much an art as it is a science'.

## A.1.1  Frequency of use

The full results are presented in Table A.1. One limitation of this table is that it does not recognise that certain valuation methodologies are more appropriate to companies in certain sectors. For example, several respondents pointed out that property companies are valued primarily on the basis of appraised net asset value.

The most frequently cited 'other' valuation method was an enterprise value/Earnings Before Interest, Tax, Depreciation and Amortisation (*EBITDA*) or enterprise value/ Earnings Before Interest and Tax (*EBIT*) ratio. Over 10% of respondents mentioned it.

*Table A.1* Valuation methodology.

| Rank | Method | Mean score | Standard deviation | 1 (%) | 2 (%) | 3 (%) | 4 (%) | 5 (%) |
|---|---|---|---|---|---|---|---|---|
| 1 | Trading multiples of companies in the industry | 4.59 | 0.69 | 0 | 2 | 6 | 23 | 69 |
| 2 | Capitalisation of forecast earnings | 4.34 | 1.02 | 4 | 4 | 8 | 25 | 60 |
| 3 | Trading multiples of companies taken over (exit multiples) | 4.21 | 1.04 | 2 | 8 | 10 | 28 | 53 |
| 4 | Price/EBIT | 4.12 | 1.12 | 4 | 5 | 18 | 21 | 52 |
| 5 | Capitalisation of historic earnings | 4.03 | 1.16 | 4 | 10 | 14 | 26 | 47 |
| 6 | DCF | 3.85 | 1.08 | 2 | 11 | 24 | 28 | 35 |
| 7 | Acquisition premia | 3.52 | 1.24 | 7 | 15 | 23 | 28 | 26 |
| 8 | Industry 'rule of thumb' | 3.07 | 1.12 | 11 | 14 | 43 | 20 | 12 |
| 9 | Internal Rate of Return (*IRR*) | 3.01 | 1.24 | 14 | 19 | 33 | 20 | 14 |
| 10 | Dividend yield | 2.87 | 1.22 | 14 | 27 | 29 | 19 | 12 |
| 11 | Other | 2.59 | 1.74 | 50 | 0 | 14 | 14 | 22 |
| 12 | Historic book value | 2.07 | 1.27 | 46 | 24 | 14 | 9 | 7 |
| 13 | Liquidation value | 1.93 | 0.89 | 36 | 41 | 17 | 5 | 1 |
| 14 | Replacement cost asset value | 1.72 | 0.81 | 47 | 37 | 14 | 1 | 1 |
| 15 | Real options | 1.58 | 0.81 | 57 | 32 | 7 | 2 | 1 |

# A.1.2   Calculation of final valuation or value range

The second set of questions dealt with the way in which the respondents weighted the results of different methods. Over 70% of respondents usually or almost always placed the greatest weight on one method and used others as a check.

A number of respondents indicated that their reliance on different methods depended on the nature of the assignment. For example, one suggested that relative valuation methods were more important in flotations and other capital markets transactions, while DCFs were more important in the case of acquisitions.

Finally, a number of respondents stated that 'gut feel',

*Table A.2*   Importance of methods.

| Method | First choice (*n* = 86) (%) | Second choice (*n* = 34) (%) | Third choice (*n* = 16) (%) | Total top 3 picks (%) |
|---|---|---|---|---|
| DCF | 29.1 | 23.5 | 25.0 | 27.2 |
| Trading multiples | 25.6 | 26.5 | 18.8 | 25.0 |
| Price/EBIT | 17.4 | 2.9 | — | 11.8 |
| Capitalisation of forecast earnings | 14.0 | 14.7 | 18.8 | 14.7 |
| Capitalisation of historic earnings | 8.1 | 11.8 | 6.3 | 8.8 |

*n* = Number of respondents.

'market feel' or 'a sense of what was reasonable' were important influences on the final valuation or valuation range.

We attempted to determine which methods financiers most relied upon. Not all respondents provided an answer to this question, nor did they all provide three responses. The DCF method was highly ranked despite its rank of sixth in the frequency of use table. The question asked was: 'On which of the methodologies listed above in Section A do you typically place the most weight?'

# A.2   DISCOUNTED CASH FLOWS

There are a number of DCF approaches which vary in their ease of calculation and applicability. The survey asked respondents which of four possible approaches they used.

## A.2.1   DCF approaches

The first alternative discounts the pre-interest after-tax cash flows at the Weighted Average Cost of Capital (*WACC*) assuming a constant debt–equity ratio (the WACC method). This is the most frequently used approach in the UK with 63% of respondents using it usually or almost always.

The second approach discounts the cash flows available to shareholders (i.e., after interest and principal repayments) using the cost of equity as the discount rate – the *Equity Cash Flow (ECF)* method. This is typically used in situations where the company's initial gearing is very high. The cost of equity is recalculated each year as the gearing level decreases.

Economic profit – also referred to as residual income, Economic Value Added *(EVA)* or Shareholder Value Added *(SVA)* – is forecast and discounted at the WACC (Shareholder Value Method). There is no benefit to be gained in using this method for valuation – its greatest use is in providing an annual snapshot of corporate economic performance.

Finally, Adjusted Present Value *(APV)* separately values operating cash flows and the tax shields provided by interest payments using different discount rates. APV probably provides the most useful approach in complex valuation situations as it disaggregates the sources of value.


## A.2.2   Forecast period

The length of the cash flow forecast was also investigated. A wide range of responses was recorded (from 2.5 to 20 years). Some of the variance can be explained by the industry specialities of the respondent. Those covering utilities and other relatively stable industries indicated a longer cash flow forecast than others. The most frequent response was 5 years, although the average was 7.14 years and the median 7.0 years.

Table A.3   DCF method.

| Rank | Method | Mean score | Standard deviation | 1 (%) | 2 (%) | 3 (%) | 4 (%) | 5 (%) |
|------|--------|-----------|--------------------|-------|-------|-------|-------|-------|
| 1 | WACC | 3.71 | 1.38 | 11 | 11 | 15 | 23 | 40 |
| 2 | ECF | 2.59 | 1.42 | 33 | 19 | 15 | 22 | 11 |
| 3 | Shareholder value | 2.34 | 1.29 | 37 | 20 | 20 | 17 | 6 |
| 4 | Adjusted Present Value (APV) | 2.04 | 1.18 | 44 | 25 | 18 | 8 | 4 |

## A.2.3   Terminal value

An extremely important component of any cash flow based valuation is the calculation of the terminal value at the end of the explicit cash flow forecast. Depending on the length of the forecast period, the terminal value estimate can often provide more than half of the total value ascribed to the company.

The most frequent response – multiple of earnings or EBIT in the final year – is unfortunately not theoretically correct. It mixes an accounting measure (with its limitations) with an economic measure of cash flow. The corporate financier is making assumptions about the multiple which is achievable in the future.

Interestingly, the method currently favoured by many strategy consultants – the 'hold and fade' method – was cited very infrequently. 'Hold and fade' is a refinement of the perpetuity calculation. The method recognises that a company's cash flows are highly unlikely to increase in perpetuity or that it will be able to continue

*Table A.4*   Terminal value calculation.

| Rank | Method | Mean score | Standard deviation | 1 (%) | 2 (%) | 3 (%) | 4 (%) | 5 (%) |
|------|--------|------------|--------------------|-------|-------|-------|-------|-------|
| 1 | Multiple of final year earnings or EBIT | 3.45 | 1.27 | 13 | 8 | 21 | 37 | 21 |
| 2 | Value of perpetuity | 2.95 | 1.33 | 23 | 11 | 27 | 27 | 12 |
| 3 | Value of a growing perpetuity | 2.78 | 1.48 | 29 | 16 | 20 | 18 | 18 |
| 4 | Hold and fade | 2.16 | 1.25 | 43 | 20 | 19 | 12 | 5 |

to earn a return greater than its cost of capital indefinitely. Therefore, it suggests a period of time when the company continues to earn a return in excess of its cost of capital (typically up to 7 years), then gradually reducing (fading) its return on invested capital to equal its cost of capital.

# A.3   COST OF CAPITAL

One of the most important contributors to 'value' is the choice of the discount rate used in determining the present value of cash flows. Most debate is generated by the calculation of the cost of equity as the calculation of the cost of debt is relatively straightforward.

## A.3.1   Determining the cost of equity

Several methods are available for calculating the cost of equity. The dividend discount model, Capital Asset

Table A.5  Determining the cost of equity.

| Rank | Method | Mean score | Standard deviation | 1 (%) | 2 (%) | 3 (%) | 4 (%) | 5 (%) |
|---|---|---|---|---|---|---|---|---|
| 1 | CAPM | 3.67 | 1.43 | 14 | 7 | 15 | 23 | 40 |
| 2 | Risk free rate + Assumed risk premium for the particular stock | 3.01 | 1.42 | 21 | 18 | 19 | 23 | 19 |
| 3 | Dividend discount model | 1.99 | 1.03 | 39 | 34 | 19 | 6 | 3 |
| 4 | Other | 1.42 | 1.12 | 86 | 3 | 3 | 2 | 7 |

Pricing Model (*CAPM*), Arbitrage Pricing Model (*APM*) and option approaches are the most commonly taught in business schools. The CAPM continues to be the most used in practice. Each has limitations either with respect to the ease of calculation (APM) or the inability of empirical testing to validate the theory (CAPM).

## A.3.2  Capital asset pricing model

Several questions were asked regarding the components of the formula: the risk-free rate of interest, the company's beta, and the equity risk premium (the return on the equity market in excess of the risk-free return that is required by equity investors)

$$K_e = r_f + \beta(r_m - r_f)$$

The CAPM has been subject to extensive theoretical and empirical examination. These studies indicate that

CAPM (and specifically the beta factor) may not be the best measure of calculating the cost of equity and that other factors such as book to market values and firm size may be better indicators of expected equity returns. However, CAPM remains in widespread use, partly because of the wide availability of published betas (see Table A.8) and its continued acceptance by practitioners as noted above. In addition, none of the alternatives has proven to be without limitations.

### A.3.2.1   Risk-free rate of return

Responses to the question of the source of the risk-free rate of return overwhelmingly favoured medium-/long-term government bonds.

*Table A.6*   Risk-free rate.

| Rank | Rate used | Respondents (%) |
|------|-----------|-----------------|
| 1 | Medium-/long-term government bonds | 80.5 |
| 2 | Short-term government bills | 13.9 |
| 3 | Other | 5.5 |

### A.3.2.2   Beta

One of the main reasons for the continued widespread use of the CAPM is the wide range of sources that publish betas for individual companies. This is illustrated by the almost equal reliance on the top three beta sources: London Business School, Datastream and Bloomberg.

Table A.7   Sources of beta.

| Rank | Source | Respondents using (%) |
|------|--------|----------------------|
| 1 | London Business School Risk Measurement Service | 26.8 |
| 2 | Datastream | 25.3 |
| 3 | Bloomberg | 22.1 |
| 4 | Barra | 10.5 |
| 5 | Internal calculation | 9.5 |
| 6 | Other | 3.7 |
| 7 | Use beta of 1.0 for all | 2.1 |

### A.3.2.3   Equity Risk Premium

The Equity Risk Premium (ERP) has been the subject of significant academic and practitioner debate in recent years. Traditionally, bankers and analysts had relied upon historic excess returns as a proxy for future returns. It was believed that accurate forecasts of equity market returns were impossible to obtain, therefore a long-run average of excess returns was an appropriate proxy for future expected returns.

Studies in both the UK and the US found that, over the long run (1920–1994), equities provided a return of approximately 8.3% above the risk-free rate (as calculated using an arithmetic mean). When the returns were calculated on the basis of a geometric mean (i.e., to take account of compounding) the historic equity risk premium dropped to between 5.0% and 5.50% leading to a debate over whether the returns should be calculated on an arithmetic or geometric basis.

Corporate finance texts line up on both sides of the issue. Brealey & Myers' *Principles of Corporate Finance* advocates the use of the arithmetic mean, while others (including Copeland *et al.*, 2000) recommend the geometric mean. Table A.8 indicates the methods used by practitioners to calculate the ERP. The final column indicates the UK risk premium as calculated by each method.

*Table A.8*   Calculation of Equity Risk Premium.

| Rank | Method | Respondents (%) | UK Equity Risk Premium |
|------|--------|-----------------|------------------------|
| 1 | Forward looking | 52.0 | 5.05 |
| 2 | Historic average (arithmetic mean) | 26.5 | 5.46 |
| 3 | Historic average (geometric mean) | 18.6 | 4.59 |
| 4 | Other | 14.7 | NA |

*Note*: The total sums to more than 100 because 12 respondents gave multiple answers.

Table A.9 summarises the results of the current ERP in use in the UK. Many respondents entered a range rather than a single number. When this occurred, we used the midpoint of the range in calculating the mean and standard deviation.

*Table A.9* UK Equity Risk Premium.

| Country | n | Mean | Mode | Standard deviation | Minimum (%) | Maximum (%) |
|---------|-----|------|------|----------|---------|---------|
| UK | 52 | 4.87 | 4.0 | 1.68 | 2 | 10 |

n = Number of responses; Mode = Most frequent response.

# SOURCES OF INFORMATION

The survey also requested respondents to indicate the publicly available sources of information used while undertaking valuations. Clearly, management forecasts and interviews would be very highly ranked if they had been included in the question. Published financial statements and brokers' reports were viewed as the most valuable sources of information (see Table A.10).

*Table A.10* Sources of information.

| Rank | Source | Median score | Standard deviation |
|------|--------|--------------|--------------------|
| 1 | Annual report and accounts | 4.77 | 0.65 |
| 2 | Interim reports | 4.40 | 0.96 |
| 3 | Brokers' reports (other firms') | 4.21 | 1.01 |
| 4 | Consensus earnings estimates | 4.17 | 1.04 |
| 5 | Brokers' reports (own firm) | 3.97 | 1.47 |
| 6 | Other | 3.71 | 1.72 |
| 7 | Financial press | 3.40 | 1.28 |
| 8 | Trade journals | 2.96 | 1.27 |
| 9 | Consultants' reports | 2.83 | 1.12 |
| 10 | Government statistics | 2.77 | 1.11 |
| 11 | Internet (World Wide Web) | 2.75 | 1.33 |

Two categories of brokers' reports were included: own firm and other firms. The reason that other firms' reports ranks higher than own firm is a consequence of the number of respondents working for merchant banks, corporate finance boutiques or accounting firms with no research or broking capacity.

Within the financial statements, the numeric presentation of the results was deemed to be more important than the descriptive, narrative sections.

*Table A.11*  Content of annual report and accounts.

| Rank | Source | Median score | Standard deviation |
|---|---|---|---|
| 1 | Income statement/profit and loss | 4.84 | 0.46 |
| 2 | Balance sheet | 4.76 | 0.62 |
| 3 | Cash flow statement | 4.62 | 0.79 |
| 4 | Operating and financial review | 3.91 | 1.10 |
| 5 | Chairman's statement | 3.41 | 1.38 |
| 6 | Directors' report | 3.30 | 1.42 |

# GLOSSARY

........................................

**Adjusted Present Value (APV)**  A project or corporate valuation method that separates the components of the project's value into its operational value and the value of its financing side-effects.

**American Depository Receipts (ADRs)**  Certificates issued by a bank stating that a specific number of a company's shares have been deposited with it. These certificates are denominated in dollars and traded on American exchanges as if they were American securities. However, ADRs represent stock in companies outside America.

**Allotment letter**  Allocation of shares from a **New issue** is made by means of an allotment letter. This entitles the recipient to a certain number of shares, subject to payment. When demand for a new issue exceeds the shares available, allotment is made either on a random (*see* **Ballot**) or proportional basis.

**Allotment price**  Price at which stock is allotted to successful applicants in a **New issue** or other offer.

**Alternative Investment Market (AIM)**  AIM was established in 1995 as a market for companies unable to join the **Official List** of the London Stock Exchange. It has less onerous requirements for listing than the Official List.

**American option**  An **Option** which may be exercised any time between its initiation and expiration dates (inclusive).

**Annualised return**  The rate of return for any given period expressed as the equivalent average return per year.

**Arbitrage**  Seeking to exploit price differences between different markets in similar instruments. An early example of arbitrage was between the dollar/sterling market in New York and that in London. Because prices in the two markets sometimes differed, traders could occasionally buy dollars or pounds in one market and sell them immediately in the other for a profit.

**Asset stripping**  A process by which a controlling shareholder sells the assets of a company and pays the proceeds to the shareholders (often himself). Alternatively, the cash proceeds are retained within the remaining 'shell' of the original company to be used for a variety of purposes.

**Authorised capital**  The amount of share capital that a limited company is authorised to issue. This does not provide any indication of the worth of the company which is related to its **Issued capital** and reserves, its net asset value and its profitability.

**Ballot**  When a **New issue** is over-subscribed some or all of the applications may be 'put into a hat' and applications drawn at random to be granted part or all of the shares applied for. Applications not selected are unsuccessful and are returned.

**Basis point**  One hundredth of 1% (i.e., 0.01%).

**Beta**  A measurement of market sensitivity – i.e., the extent to which a share or portfolio fluctuates with the market. It is a statistical estimate, based on historical data, of the average percentage of change in a fund or a security's rate of return corresponding to a 1% change in the stock market.

**Bond**  A certificate of debt issued by a company, government or other institution. A bondholder is a creditor of the issuer and receives interest at a rate stated at the time of issue.

**Bond ratings**  A system for measuring the relative creditworthiness of bond issues using rating symbols, which range from the highest investment quality (least investment risk) to below investment grade (greatest risk).

**Bonus issue**  When a company issues extra shares free of charge to existing shareholders on a *pro rata* basis. Compare with **Rights issue**.

**Call**  A payment on a specified date on a **Partly paid** stock, to be paid by the holder of the **Allotment letter**.

**Call option**  An **Option** that gives the buyer the right (but not the obligation) to buy a specified quantity of the underlying instrument at a fixed price, on or before a specified date. Compare with **Put option.**

**Capital Asset Pricing Model (CAPM)** Sophisticated model of the relationship between expected risk and expected return. Grounded in the theory that investors require higher returns for higher risks.

**Capitalisation issue** An issue creating additional share capital either by the issue of new shares for old as with a **Scrip** issue or by share rationalisation.

**Chinese Walls** Controls over communications between corporate financiers, on the one hand, and researchers, traders and salesmen, on the other, in integrated securities houses to avoid potential conflicts of interest.

**Comfort letter** Letter given by a professional advisor to a company supporting statements that have been made in listing particulars or offering circular.

**Convertible stock** Stock which gives the holder the right, but not the obligation, to convert all or part of the holding into another stock or stocks on specified dates and on specified terms. Forms include convertible bonds, convertible debentures and convertible preference shares.

**Corporate governance** Issues relating to the way in which a company ensures that it is attaching maximum importance to the interests of its shareholders and how shareholders can influence management.

**Cum dividend** **Cum** is the Latin prefix meaning 'with'. A share quoted cum dividend carries the right to a recently declared dividend. Cum scrip and cum rights have similar meanings. Compare with **Ex dividend**.

**Dawn raid** Term for an investor (corporate raider) buying a substantial number of a company's shares before the market becomes aware of its intentions. The buyer's objective is usually to build a strategic stake in the target company and often leads to a full takeover bid.

**Debenture** A **Bond** backed by a prior claim on the assets of the issuer or, in some circumstances, by specific assets of the issuer. A debenture holder is entitled to appoint a receiver if necessary.

**dividend** The part of a company's after-tax earnings which is distributed to the shareholders in the form of cash or shares. The directors of the company decide how much dividend is to be paid and when. A dividend is neither automatic nor guaranteed for ordinary shareholders.

**Dividend discount model**   A model for determining the price of a security based on the discounted value of its projected future dividend payments.

**Dividend cover**   The extent to which the **Dividends** distributed by a company are backed by the distributable earnings of the company (net profit after tax divided by total dividends).

**Dividend yield**   The return that the annual **Dividend** of a share represents in relation to the current share price. Calculated by dividing the annual dividend per share by the current market price.

**Earnings per share**   A common way of expressing company profits – dividing the profit after tax by the number of shares in issue.

**Equity**   The capital of a company belonging to the **Ordinary shareholders** who have voting rights allowing them to influence the management of the company.

**Equity risk premium**   The difference between the rate of return available from the risk-free asset (government bonds) and that available from ordinary shares, which are a more volatile investment.

**Ex dividend**   To clarify who receives the **Dividend** on a share that is sold around the time the dividend is due, a date is fixed when a share goes ex dividend. Anyone buying after this date will not receive the dividend. A share price will normally fall by the amount of the dividend on the day that it goes ex dividend. Compare with **Cum dividend.**

**Exercise price**   The price at which an option holder has the right to buy or sell the underlying asset. Also referred to as 'strike price'.

**Expiry date**   The last date on which an option can be exercised. Also referred to as **Maturity date**.

**Face value**   The value of a bond that appears on the bond certificate, unless the value is otherwise specified by the issuer. Face value is ordinarily the amount the issuer promises to pay at maturity and is not an indication of the current market value. Also called **Par value**.

**Financial Services Authority (FSA)**   The leading financial regulatory agency in the UK. Sets out policy and governs the content of **New issue prospectuses**. Similar functions to the **SEC**.

**Fixed interest**   An income stream which remains constant during the life of the asset, such as income derived from **Bonds**, annuities and **Preference shares**.

**Flotation**   The first issue of shares to the public in a company new to the stock market. *See* **Initial public offering.**

**FT All-Share Index**   An arithmetically weighted index of leading UK shares (by market capitalisation) listed on the London Stock Exchange. The FTSE 100 Index (or 'Footsie') covers only the largest 100 companies.

**Fully paid**   Shares on which the full nominal value has been subscribed. Compare with **Nil paid** and **Partly paid.**

**Fundamental analysis**   Analysis of share values based on factors such as sales, earnings and assets that are 'fundamental' to the enterprise of the company in question. These factors are considered in light of current share prices to ascertain any mispricing of the shares.

**GAAP**   Generally Accepted Accounting Principles, as set by national (e.g., UK, US) or international (e.g., IAS) regulators.

**Gearing**   A measure of how much a company has borrowed.

**Gilts, gilt-edged securities**   Sterling-denominated **Bonds** issued by the British government.

**Greenmail**   A term that describes the situation when a hostile bidder threatens a company with takeover by purchasing a large number of its shares, forcing the management of the company to repurchase those shares at an above-market price. (Occurred mainly in the 1980s in the US.)

**Grey market**   The familiar name given to the unofficial market for a new security before its formal offering. Also known as 'when issued trading'.

**Impact day**   The date on which the FSA approves the entry of the issue to the **Official List** and when the underwriting of the issue takes place.

**Initial Public Offering (IPO)**   The first sale of shares of a company to the public. Also referred to as **Flotation.**

**Interest cover**   A measure of a company's ability to meet its interest obligations, calculated by dividing EBIT by interest payments. The higher the ratio the better.

**Interest rate risk**   The risk borne by fixed interest securities, and by borrowers with floating rate loans, when interest rates fluctuate. When interest rates rise, the market value of fixed interest securities declines and *vice versa.*

**Introduction**   An application for a listing on the stock exchange when the shares to be listed are already widely held by the public.

**Issued capital**   The portion of a company's **Authorised capital** that has been issued by the company.

**Issuing house**   An infrequently used term given to financial institutions, often merchant banks, that act as intermediaries between companies seeking capital and the investors prepared to supply it.

**Junk bond**   A high-risk, high-yield debt security rated below triple B.

**Listing**   For shares (or **Bonds**) to be traded officially on a stock market they need to be listed. Essentially, this is an endorsement from the market authorities that the securities and their issuer meet certain criteria.

**Listing particulars**   Detailed information that must be published by a company applying to be listed. The content is guided by the **Purple Book**.

**Listing rules**   Rule book for listed companies. Was commonly referred to as the **Yellow Book**, but since the change in regulatory responsibility in 2000 from the London Stock Exchange to the Financial Services Authority, known as the **Purple Book** after the colour of its cover.

**Loan stock**   Another name for a **Bond**, normally used in connection with those issued by non-government bodies such as companies.

**Long-form report**   Detailed report on the company and its business prepared by the reporting accountants for the company's directors and the **Sponsor** of a **New issue.**

**Market capitalisation**   The result of the number of ordinary shares issued by a corporation, multiplied by the current market price of a share.

**Maturity**   End of the life of a fixed interest security at which point it is repaid. Also known as redemption. Maturity can also mean the end of the life of a future or option.

**Model code**   Rules issued by the Stock Exchange to be followed by the directors of a company when dealing in the company's shares.

**Money market**   The market for trade in short-term securities (maturity of less than 1 year) such as bills of exchange, promissory notes and Government **Treasury bills (T-bills).**

**Net present value**   The current value of a stream of income discounted by a factor over the period of an investment.

**New issue** New shares issued by companies to raise additional cash. Can refer to an **Initial public offering** or a **Rights issue** (secondary offering).

**Nil paid** Shares whose nominal value has not been paid up and where there is therefore a **Call** due on the balance. Government stocks (bonds) are sometimes issued in this way, with one or more calls at specified dates.

**Nominal rate of return** A rate of return expressed only in monetary terms. Compare with **Real rate** of return.

**Nominal value** Sometimes known as par value, this is the face value of a security as opposed to its market value. In the case of a **Bond** it represents the principal sum due on redemption.

**Off balance sheet** Referring to financial commitments or liabilities that do not generally appear in a company's balance sheet.

**Offer for sale** One of the means by which a company can be floated, where the **Sponsor** offers shares to the public.

**Official List** The main portion of the London Stock Exchange with approximately 2,000 companies quoted. Complemented by the **Alternative Investment Market** for smaller companies and OFEX which offers a trading service for companies whose shares trade very infrequently.

**Options** The right to buy (**Call option**) or sell (**Put option**) a specific security at a specified price, at or within a specified time, whatever happens to its market price. This right can usually only be obtained by payment of an amount (known as the premium) to the writer of the option.

**Ordinary shares** Securities which represent an ownership interest in a company. If the company has also issued **Preference shares**, both have ownership rights.

**Over-subscription** A new issue is said to be over-subscribed when more applications are received than there are shares for offer. In this event, applications are scaled down *pro rata* or offered by a ballot. *See* **Allotment letter** and **Ballot**.

**Over the counter (OTC)** A financial contract that is not traded on an exchange but is 'tailor-made' for a client by a financial institution.

**Par value** *See* **Nominal value**.

**Partly paid** Shares or bonds may be issued partly paid, meaning that the full value of the investment will be paid in two or more instalments or **Calls**. Only the first instalment is paid on issue.

**Pathfinder prospectus** Draft prospectus (preliminary) published in advance of pricing of the offering to aid in marketing the **New issue.**

**PE ratio** Price–earnings ratio. A ratio used to value a company's shares. It is calculated by dividing the current market price by the earnings per share.

**Placing** The placing of a company's securities made by a **Sponsor** or stockbroker with its own clients and with the market.

**Placing agreement** Terms under which the **Sponsor** agrees to underwrite the placing of the company's shares to its clients. *See* **Underwriting agreement.**

**POS regulations** Public Offers of Securities regulations (1995) are the regulations governing all offers of securities other than those to be listed on the **Official List**.

**Preference share** Preference shares rank before **Ordinary shares** in respect of **Dividend** payments and, usually, capital repayment. Dividends on preference shares are at a fixed rate and the shares do not normally carry voting rights unless the dividend is in arrears.

**Present value** The current value of an investment which matures in the future, after discounting the maturity at an assumed rate of interest and adjusting for the probability of its payment or receipt.

**Primary market** The market in which securities are sold at the time they are first issued.

**Promissory note** A debt security issued by a borrower, showing the amount that the borrower is prepared to pay the noteholder on its maturity. The note is issued at a discount to its face value, representing the yield on the funds for the noteholder.

**Prospectus** A legal document setting out the terms of issue of a new stock. The published document containing all the details of offer for sale or placing, which can also be called the **Listing particulars**. *See* **New issue**.

**Put option** An **Option** that gives the buyer the right (but not the obligation) to sell a specified quantity of the underlying instrument at a fixed price, on or before a specified date. The writer (seller) of the option has the obligation to take delivery of the underlying instrument if the option is exercised by the buyer. Compare with **Call option.**

**Real rate of return**  Nominal rate of return adjusted for inflation.

**Red herring**  A US term for a preliminary prospectus issued in advance of the offer. *See* **Pathfinder prospectus.**

**Rights issue**  When existing shareholders are given rights to purchase new shares in proportion to their existing holding. Compare with **Bonus issue.**

**Risk premium**  The extra **Yield** over the **Risk-free rate** demanded by investors to compensate them for the possibility of default.

**Risk-free asset/rate**  An investment with no chance of default, and a known or certain rate of return. Either **Treasury bills** or **Gilts** in the UK.

**Scrip issue**  A share issue which raises no new money for a company, but simply gives extra shares to existing holders. Also known as a bonus issue. Compare with **Rights issue.**

**Securities Exchange Commission (SEC)**  An independent regulatory agency in the US with responsibility for administering the federal securities laws. The SEC also regulates firms involved in the purchase or sale of securities, people who provide investment advice and investment companies. Similar functions to those of the **FSA.**

**Secondary market**  Any market in which existing securities are traded (as distinct from the primary market, in which securities are first issued). The Stock Exchange is the secondary market for share trading.

**Share buy-back**  Corporate self-purchase of its own shares in the market to reduce its issued share capital. Changes the proportion of debt to equity that it holds on its balance sheet.

**Share certificate**  A piece of paper representing legal evidence of ownership of a stipulated number of shares in a company. Also known as a **Scrip.**

**Short form report**  A report prepared by the reporting accountants for a **New issue**, which is included in the listing particulars, setting out the results for the last 3 years, the cash flow statements and the balance sheets.

**Small-cap**  Term used to describe the smallest listed companies on the stock exchange.

**Sponsor**  All activities and matters connected to a new issue are co-ordinated by a sponsor, which may be a merchant bank, investment bank, stockbroker or accounting firm. The sponsor is responsible for arranging the timing and underwriting of the issue and ensuring that the company is fairly portrayed in the **Prospectus.**

**Stag**  An investor in the stock market who aims for quick gains by subscribing to new share issues and then selling once the shares commence trading on the exchange.

**Subscription**  An agreement to purchase a certain offering.

**Sub-underwriting**  The sponsor (or **Underwriter**) of a **New issue** will usually spread its financial risk by sub-underwriting a proportion of its total commitment with other financial institutions.

**Takeover bid**  An offer made to the shareholders of a company by an individual or organisation intending to gain control of that company.

**Technical analysis**  An approach to the analysis of stock and futures and their future trends which examines the technical factors of market activity, often represented by charting patterns, as contrasted with **Fundamental analysis.**

**Tender**  An infrequently used method of issuing securities whereby investors are invited to bid, subject to a minimum price. The allocation of the securities is made according to the prices bid. This method can be used when comparable companies are hard to find, or when the demand for shares is anticipated to be overwhelming.

**Tender offer**  A public offer to buy some or all of the existing stock of a company within a specified period.

**Treasury bill (T-bill)**  Treasury bills are short-term debt instruments issued by the UK and other governments. Their return is derived from being issued at a discount to their final redemption value.

**Underwriter**  The underwriter (or **Sponsor**) 'insures' a **New issue** (or **Rights issue**) by agreeing to buy all shares which are not sold. The underwriter typically earns a fee of 0.5% of the funds it guarantees to underwrite.

**Underwriting agreement**  Agreement which sets out the arrangement made between the company and the **Sponsor** that the sponsor will, for a fee, purchase all shares not taken up by the public. The sponsor will usually spread its financial risk by arranging to **Sub-underwrite** the issue with major financial institutions, the sub-underwriters taking up any unsold shares.

**Unquoted securities**   Shares which are dealt in the market but which are not subject to any listing requirements and are given no official status.

**Venture capital**   Capital which is subject to more than a normal degree of risk, usually associated with a new business or venture and particularly in relation to new-technology projects.

**Verification**   Procedures undertaken to confirm the accuracy and fairness of statements made in the prospectus. Solicitors to the issue conduct detailed verification of all statements of fact and opinion in the prospectus.

**Voting rights**   **Ordinary shares** usually have associated voting rights that enable the holder to influence the management of the company. *See also* **Corporate governance.**

**Warrant**   A certificate giving the holder the right to purchase shares at a stipulated price within a specified timespan. The money paid upon exercise is received by the company issuing the warrant, unlike options, which raise no new capital.

**Working capital statement**   Statement provided by the directors of any company going public confirming that the company's working capital is adequate for the following year. Usually the reporting accountants will write a letter of comfort to the directors and **Sponsors** having reviewed the statement and its supporting evidence.

**Yield**   A **Measure** of the income return earned on an investment. In the case of a share the yield expresses the annual **Dividend** payment as a percentage of the market price of the share. In the case of a **Bond** the running yield (or **Flat yield**) is the annual interest payable as a percentage of the current market price. The redemption yield (or yield to maturity) allows for any gain or loss of capital which will be realised at the **Maturity** date.

**Yield curve**   A graphical representation of the relationship between the **Yields of bonds** with the same credit quality, but of different maturities. The Government yield curve is the basis of the pricing of new bond issues.

**Yield to maturity**   The yield provided by a bond which is held to its maturity date, taking account of both interest payments and capital gains or losses.

**Yellow Book**   Document formerly used to govern the listing requirements for the London Stock Exchange.

# ABBREVIATIONS

. . . . . . . . . . . . . . . . . . . . . . . . . . . . . . . . . . . .

| | |
|---|---|
| ADR | American Depository Receipt |
| AIM | Alternative Investment Market |
| APM | Arbitrage Pricing Model |
| APV | Adjusted Present Value |
| BA | Bankers' Acceptance |
| CAPM | Capital Asset Pricing Model |
| CFROI | Cash Flow Return on Investment |
| CP | Commercial Paper |
| DCF | Discounted Cash Flow |
| DR | Depository Receipt |
| EBIT | Earnings Before Interest and Tax |
| EBITDA | Earnings Before Interest, Tax, Depreciation and Amortisation |
| ECF | Equity Cash Flow |
| ECM | Equity Capital Market |
| ECP | EuroCommercial Paper |
| EPS | Earnings Per Share |
| ERP | Equity Risk Premium |
| EURIBOR | Euro LIBOR |
| EVA$^{TM}$ | Economic Value Added |
| FCF | Free Cash Flow |
| GDR | Global Depository Receipt |
| IBO | Institutional BuyOut |
| IPO | Initial Public Offering |
| IRR | Internal Rate of Return |
| LBO | Leveraged BuyOut |
| LIBOR | London Inter-Bank Offer Rate |
| LSE | London Stock Exchange |

| | |
|---|---|
| M&A | Mergers, Acquisitions and Divestitures |
| MBI | Management BuyIn |
| MBO | Management BuyOut |
| NASDAQ | National Association of Securities Dealers Automated Quotation system |
| NOPAT | Net Operating Profit After Tax |
| NOPLAT | Net Operating Profit Less Adjusted Taxes |
| OFT | Office of Fair Trading |
| PE | Price Earnings |
| PER | Price Earnings Ratio |
| PIK | Payment In Kind |
| QIB | Qualified Institutional Investor |
| R&D | Research and Development |
| ROCE | Return On Capital Employed |
| SEC | Securities Exchange Commission |
| SVA | Shareholder Value Added |
| T-Bill | Treasury Bill |
| UKLA | UK Listing Authority |
| US GAAP | US Generally Accepted Accounting Principles |
| VC | Venture Capitalist |
| WACC | Weighted Average Cost of Capital |

# ADDITIONAL READING

The following books are useful additions to the corporate financier's bookshelf.

Arnold, G. (1998) *Corporate Financial Management*. Financial Times/Pitman Publishing (0-273-63078-4).

Brealey, R. A. and S. C. Myers (2000) *Principles of Corporate Finance* (6th Edition). McGraw Hill (0-07-709565-0).

Burroughs, B. and J. Helyar (1991) *Barbarians at the Gate*. Arrow (0-099-82330-6).

Button, M. and S. Button (1999) *A Practitioner's Guide to the City Code on Takeovers and Mergers*. City & Financial Publishing (1-898-83033-9).

Damodaran, A. (2002) *Investment Valuation: Tools and Techniques for Determining the Value of Any Asset* (2nd Edition). John Wiley & Sons (0-471-41488-3).

Damodaran, A. (2003) *Corporate Finance: Theory and Practice* (2nd Edition, WSE). John Wiley & Sons (0-471-28332-0).

Dwyer, M. (1997) *Management Buy Outs*. Sweet & Maxwell (0-421-52670-X).

Galpin, T. J. and M. Hendon (1999) *The Complete Guide to Mergers and Acquisitions*. Jossey Bass Wiley (0-787-94786-5).

Galpin, T. J. and M. Hendon (2000) *Tolley's Company Acquisitions Handbook*. Tolley Publishing (1-860-12896-3).

Herzel, L. and R. Sheppo (1990) *Acquisitions, Mergers and Defences in the USA*. Blackwell Publishers (0-631-16422-7).

Hubbard, N. (2001) *Acquisitions*. Palgrave (0-333-94548-4).

Houghton, G. (2000) *Due Diligence*. Accountancy Books (1-853-55902-4).

Lajoux, A. R. (2000) *The Art of M&A Due Diligence*. Irwin Professional (0-786-31150-9).

McKinsey & Co. (2005) *Valuation: Measuring and Managing the Value of Companies* (4th Edition). John Wiley & Sons (0-471-70221-8).

Rappaport, A. (1998) *Creating Shareholder Value: A Guide for Investors and Managers* (2nd Edition). Free Press (0-684-84410-9).

Rivas, J. (ed.) (2000) *The EU Merger Regulation and the Anatomy of the Merger Task Force*. Kluwer Law International (9-041-19767-2).

Robbie, K. and M. Wright (1996) *Management Buy Ins*. Manchester University Press (0-719-04281-X).

Wasserstein, B. (2000) *Big Deal: 2000 and Beyond*. Time Warner (0-446-52642-8).

Weston, F. J. (2000) *A Practitioners' Guide to Takeovers and Mergers in the European Union: 1999/2000*. Cedar Tree Press (1-898-83034-7).

Weston, F. J. (2001) *Mergers and Acquisitions*. McGraw Hill (0-071-36432-3).

# INDEX